# CANCER
## OVERCOMERS

*Gold Refined By Fire*

THE THIRTEEN P's
A Scripture Study of How to Apply the Blood of the Lamb
And the Word of Your Testimony

## TRUDY BRINLING GOERK

Trilogy Christian Publishers
A Wholly Owned Subsidiary of Trinity Broadcasting Network
2442 Michelle Drive
Tustin, CA 92780

Cover design by: Cornerstone Creative Solutions

For information, address Trilogy Christian Publishing
Rights Department, 2442 Michelle Drive, Tustin, Ca 92780.
Trilogy Christian Publishing/ TBN and colophon are trademarks of Trinity Broadcasting Network.

For information about special discounts for bulk purchases, please contact Trilogy Christian Publishing.

Manufactured in the United States of America

10 9 8 7 6 5 4 3 2 1

Library of Congress Cataloging-in-Publication Data is available.

ISBN 978-1-64773-961-4 (Print Book)
ISBN 978-1-64773-962-1 (ebook)

This book is dedicated to the Hebrews Eleven Hall of Famers that have gone on before us.

Hebrews 11:13-16 (NKJV):

*These all died in faith, not having received the promises, but having seen them afar off were assured of them, embraced them and confessed that they were strangers and pilgrims on the earth. For those who say such things declare plainly that they seek a homeland. And truly if they had called to mind that country from which they had come out, they would have had opportunity to return. But now they desire a better, that is, a heavenly country. Therefore God is not ashamed to be called their God, for He has prepared a city for them.*

# CONTENTS

# INTRODUCTION

My first introduction to Trudy Goerk was her application for Youth With A Mission's Medical Discipleship Training School in Kailua-Kona, Hawaii. I was on the staff of her school, was her one-on-one, and walked with her through the discovery of a suspicious tumor and the events that led to her leaving Hawaii. Her book shares the story of her Goliath (a cancerous tumor) that she faced, the *foundation* she stood on in the battle and the *weapons of warfare* that she used during the fight. Her book is a battle plan when facing cancer, and it contains prompts to draw out individual biblical strategies for those dealing with the disease.

Donna Tredway, RN<br>
Medical Discipleship Training School<br>
Youth With A Mission<br>
Kona, Hawaii

As President of the South Carolina Faith Community Nurses Association, I am pleased to endorse *Cancer Overcomers: Gold Refined by Fire-The Thirteen P's; A Scripture Study of How to Apply the Blood of the Lamb and the Word of Your Testimony.* Faith community nursing practice focuses on the intentional care of the spirit, promotion of an integrative model of health, and prevention and minimization of illness within the context of a faith community. Such practitioners consider the spiritual, physical, psychological, and social aspects of an individual to create a sense of harmony with self, others, the environment, and a higher power.

Facing the battle of cancer is not only a physical and mental battle but also a powerful spiritual one. We are spirit, soul, and body creations living in God's creation. Trudy Goerk compassionately weaves her journey with cancer and her testimony of faith with God's Word to lead the reader through a Bible study revealing God's purpose, preparation, plan, provision, peace, presence, promises, power, protection, prosperity, perfection, performance, and prayer. This Bible study gives the reader very practical and appropriate Scriptures, leading the reader through God's healing process to achieve wholeness, His Shalom. I trust that the reader will find peace, purpose, and ultimately joy in God's Son, Jesus Christ, our Great Physician and healer. This publication is helpful not only for the person experiencing the journey through cancer treatment, but for anyone experiencing a life-limiting illness. This Bible study is also helpful for those who are supportive caregivers and a good resource for faith community nurses. Praise be to God for Trudy's five years of being cancer-free.

Donna Kleister R.N., M.S.<br>
Columbia, South Carolina

CANCER OVERCOMERS

The words you are about to read, Trudy Goerk's, are anointed with the healing balm of God Himself. I do not say this lightly and I'm not saying this because Trudy and I are friends, but because it is the truth. God has given her the passionate writing that so many writers desire. We were introduced to one another through our home church, Ember, in Chester, SC. Our sisterhood developed as our relationship deepened through membership in Word Weavers International (WWI), Charlotte, North Carolina Chapter. I am thrilled that Trudy's determination and perseverance has manifested into this authoritative power book of the 13 P's.

When you know who you are in Christ, as she definitely does, sickness cannot help but flee in Jesus name. This does not happen without the discipline of the Word being applied in daily life and seeking the true God that heals. Turning her back on God was never an option. She chose to walk in faith through it all: the loss of her husband, raising three teenagers as a single mom, working full time as a nurse, and then cancer itself. I'm proud to call Trudy my friend because it's hard, nowadays, to find sincere, honest prayer warriors that are humble enough to allow the leading of the Holy Spirit every day. This lady's the real deal, folks! God bless her always and all who take hold of this courageous teaching.

With sincere love & peace always,

Cheryl Kline Derstine
Author of Profound Paradox

...what you have done with this is just amazing.

Belinda O.
Patient with Stage IV pancreatic cancer

10

# ACKNOWLEDGMENTS

I believe it takes a village to write a book, from an embryo, idea, through development, writing, and publication, birthing; akin in many ways to raising a child.

I want to thank a few of my villagers. First, Pastor Steve Bishop, Chester Freedom Ministries, Chester, SC, in whose Bible study this book was conceived.

Chris Buehrig, a cancer survivor, who critiqued the work in process with the rare combination of loving encouragement.

My Beta-reader Linda Milligan who was brave enough to take this request on, though her husband died within four weeks of an initial cancer diagnosis. Her walk as a caregiver was brief. Revisiting this time in her life could have been very difficult. But she graciously sticky-noted comments and expressed hope that I would see this published.

The cancer patients who accepted my gift of either the full manuscript, Book One, this thirteen-week Bible study, initially intended for the ministry and health care team or Book Two, the patient booklet, *The Cancer Overcomers: Your Healing Pathway*, the condensed version designed for those undergoing active treatment. For my fellow health care workers, those who navigated me through my cancer journey in 2015, and those who have subsequently cheered me on to tell my story. I am grateful to the South Carolina Faith Community Nurses Association for their encouragement and support during both the writing process and my pursuit of publication.

And to Kevin Taylor, Pastor, Ember Church, Chester, SC, who first read the manuscript for Scriptural integrity. His thought-provoking questions and comments would linger long after I left his office, and the Holy Spirit would gently prompt me to make additional changes and revisions. Thank you, Kevin.

And to my family and intercessors, my Aaron and Hur, holding my hands up. I could not have done it without you. And a special thank you to a life-long friend, Ellen McCloskey, for archiving my 2015 emails even before I knew I had a story to tell. Pastor Kevin called these, *My Story*, "the gold" of *Cancer Overcomers*. And if gold, I would only add, gold refined by fire.

And most of all, to God be the glory! Great things He has done.

Love and blessings,
Trudy

# READERS' GUIDE

Hebrews 4:12-13 reads: "His powerful Word is sharp as a surgeon's scalpel, cutting through everything, whether doubt or defense, laying us open to listen and obey. Nothing and no one is impervious to God's Word" (The Message).

What a powerful verse to begin *Cancer Overcomers: Gold Refined by Fire, The Thirteen P's*. I believe the Bible is the inspired word of God. Inspiration in the natural, drawing air into the lungs is the very breath of life. In Genesis 2:7 "…the Lord formed man of dust from the ground, and breathed into his nostrils the very breath of life; and man became a living being." God has in-Spirited the Bible, as His very Word, living and active.

The Scripture references herein are from many varied translations, but unless otherwise designated, the New American Standard is used. Please feel free always to follow along with your favorite translation beside you, comfort food, hopefully with underlined and dog-eared pages, for our healing journey. If you don't yet own a Bible, my hope is that these diverse verses may introduce you to your next best forever friend. If you have internet access, you can download one as an application.

The study is designed to be read in chapter order, one through thirteen, followed by the epilogue. I am praying for you that the person of the Holy Spirit be your Teacher. Allow Him to set your pace regarding how much time you spend on each chapter and how much you read per day or week. On a treatment day, your patients or congregants may need encouragement from the Word earlier in the day when they are rested and before side-effects. Another day, treatment-free perhaps, their priority may be relaxation; possibly then, an evening time for prayer and study may suit them better. Adjust it to their needs and schedule. Yes, it is a study, to be meditated upon, absorbed slowly, and even committed to memory in portions as our growing armory. As you read, listen for His promptings. If you are a note-taker, you may want a journal alongside to accompany you on this study, as simple perhaps as a three-ring binder and loose-leaf paper. There will also be some spaces included throughout chapters to record your thoughts and feelings. If you find concepts in chapters that are new to you, allow the Holy Spirit to sift and sort them. They may be for you, but at a later time along your healing path. This study invites you to look at the healing Christ at work throughout the four gospels, Matthew, Mark, Luke, and John in the New Testament, and types and shadows of Him as foretold in the Old Testament. The meaning of the Hebrew names of God, Father, Son, and Holy Spirit will be a unifying thread throughout the book. And I have told *My Story*, my healing journey, in part as emails to my intercessors. Journaling has been a part of my healing process, and hopefully yours as you are introduced to it.

# PROLOGUE

I am a cancer survivor. Looking back, years before I was diagnosed, I can see God's fingerprints on my life preparing me for that very battle that lie ahead, unseen. Yes, unseen by me, but not by Him. There is a battle plan. He carefully unfolded it for me. And He can do that for you, too. May I be your or your loved one's guide? If so, dear reader, accompany me on that journey now. Let's begin.

I've found thirteen principles, all words beginning with the letter "P," that can accompany us in our Cancer Battle Plan.

The Thirteen P's are:

(1) His Purpose;
(2) His Preparation;
(3) His Plan;
(4) His Provision;
(5) His Peace;
(6) His Presence;
(7) His Promises;
(8) His Power;
(9) His Protection;
(10) His Prosperity;
(11) His Perfection;
(12) His Performance;
(13) His Prayer.

You, too, are going on a journey, a cancer battle, yourself or with a patient newly diagnosed, perhaps a congregant and family. I want to encourage you, give you courage. Each of us who embarks with God on a healing journey charts an individual path, like fingerprints. There are certain guiding principles I've learned in my own battle that highlight God's fingerprints. The how, and when, and where God applies them will be your/their unique healing story.

My prayer is that the Word of God will stir faith; Scripture memorization verses will grow faith. And combined with revelation knowledge of the love of Jesus Christ Himself, as evidenced by His own compassionate healing ministry, His suffering and death, that healing in your own or your loved ones' lives will be manifested.

In April 2012, I was part of a trip to Old Salem. I walked the very grounds the Moravians walked, under the heavens that they bombarded with worship and intercession for one hundred continuous years! The Moravians were German immigrants who founded a Protestant denomination. They originated in the fifteenth century but experienced revitalization in 1727 under Count Nicholas von Zinzendorf. "Zinzendorf was one of the wealthiest, and could have been one of the most powerful men in Europe during his time, but he esteemed being in the ministry as a higher calling, and spent his entire fortune on the gospel. Historians have called him 'the rich young ruler who said '*yes*'[1]…and he became the true father of modern missions.'"[2]

The most famous Moravian colony was the one I visited in Winston-Salem, NC. Bethabara, the original and more primitive site, and Old Salem, their main establishment and base in the Wachovia land tract (which means "a fruitful field"), are about fifteen minutes apart. Each offered significance to my journey.

As I stepped back in time walking the over six and one-half to seven block length, by three block depth, the working life of the village came alive before my eyes, with the accompanying sounds and smells: the operational German bakery, the gunsmith shop where I stood spellbound watching a re-enactment of rifle building, the blacksmith and stables, and the vast organic gardens.

But my memory highlight of that trip was kneeling in the small cemetery, God's Acre, beside tombstones and asking for mantles that have fallen to the earth and not been picked up yet. I had come on that trip fasting, expectant of spiritual food. It would be five years later that I would see exactly how God had answered my prayers. The thirteen chapters that follow are the new unfolding of this. First, let's look at the concept of mantles both in the natural and the supernatural.

Webster defines a mantle as "a loose sleeveless cloak…something that covers, envelops, or conceals… or a chemically prepared, incombustible network hood for a gas jet or kerosene wick which when the jet or wick is lighted, becomes incandescent and gives off a brilliant light."

My battle with cancer in 2015 could have been a mantle of darkness. It was not. God cloaked me with His light, and the heat of radiation, even the slow post-surgery recovery process, could not overcome His love which burned brightly as that kerosene wick. Prior, my life mantra had been Isaiah 42:3: "A bruised reed He will not break and a dimly burning wick He will not extinguish…"

To understand this gift more fully, I studied the story in 2 Kings 2:1-14:

> And it came about when the Lord was about to take up Elijah by a whirlwind to heaven, that Elijah went with Elisha from Gilgal. 2 Elijah said to Elisha, 'Stay here please, for the Lord has sent me as far as Bethel.' But Elisha said, 'As the Lord lives and as you yourself live, I will not leave you.' So, they went down to Bethel. 3 Then the sons of the prophets who were at Bethel came out to Elisha and said to him, 'Do you know that the Lord will take away your master from over you today?' And he said, 'Yes, I know; be still.'
>
> 4 Elijah said to him, 'Elisha, please stay here, for the Lord has sent me to Jericho.' But he said, 'As the Lord lives, and as you yourself live, I will not leave you.' So they came to Jericho. 5 The sons of the prophets who were at Jericho approached Elisha and said to him, 'Do you know that the Lord will take away your master from over you today?' And he answered, 'Yes, I know; be still.'
>
> 6 Then Elijah said to him, 'Please stay here, for the Lord has sent me to the Jordan.' And he said, 'As the Lord lives, and as you yourself live, I will not leave you.' So the two of them went on.
>
> 7 Now fifty men of the sons of the prophets went and stood opposite them at a distance, while the two of them stood by the Jordan. 8 Elijah took his mantle and folded it together and struck the waters, and they were divided here and there, so that the two of them crossed over on dry ground.
>
> 9 When they had crossed over, Elijah said to Elisha, 'Ask what I shall do for you before I am taken from you.' And Elisha said, 'Please, let a double portion of your spirit be upon me.' 10 He said, 'You have asked a hard thing. Nevertheless, if you see me when I am taken from you, it shall be so for you; but if not, it shall not be so.' 11 As they were going along and talking, behold, there appeared a chariot of fire and horses of fire which separated the two of them. And Elijah went up by a whirlwind to heaven. 12 Elisha saw it and cried out, 'My father, my father, the chariots of Israel and its horsemen!' And he

saw Elijah no more. Then he took hold of his own clothes and tore them in two pieces. 13 He also took up the mantle of Elijah that fell from him and returned and stood by the bank of the Jordan. 14 He took the mantle of Elijah that fell from him and struck the waters and said, 'Where is the Lord, the God of Elijah?' And when he also had struck the waters, they were divided here and there; and Elisha crossed over.

In this story, the mantle of Elijah has fallen to the ground. What did Elisha have to do to receive it? (2 Kings 2: 9)

_____

_____

Yes, first ask. But Elijah attaches a condition. Why? (2 Kings 2:10)

_____

_____

Because Elisha has "asked a hard thing." What was this hard thing asked? (2 Kings 2:9)

_____

_____

A double portion of another's mantle was a hard thing to obtain. What was the next condition attached? (2 Kings 2:10)

_____

_____

To amplify the previous definition of mantle, what is a mantle in a spiritual sense? One definition that I love is "an authority, a power, a gift, and a call."[3] How does one get a spiritual mantle?

_____

_____

Yes, ask. Simply ask God in faith in Jesus' name for one of His choosing. I believe His answer contingent upon if and when He sees you are prepared and ready to give Him all the glory. And if a mantle has already fallen to earth, one must do something further after asking: pick it up, as did Elisha (2 Kings 2:13).

And we will find more about mantles as we visit authority, power, gift, and call by looking at the healing Christ at work in the four gospels, Matthew, Mark, Luke, and John in the New Testament and types and shadows of Him as foretold in the Old Testament.

We're ready now to begin our study of the thirteen "P"s.

# CHAPTER ONE

---

## The first "P" is for *His Purpose.*

Philippians 3:10:
"…that I may know Him…"

---

His purpose for my life, your life, is that we know Him. Our love and service will flow proportional to the height and breadth and depth of that knowledge. Together, as we study the Word, Jesus (John 1:1), and His Word, the Scriptures, may our knowledge and love of Him grow.

How do we come to know Him? How did you?

_____

_____

You may have answered:

- A friend, family member, or a church introduced us.
- A Bible or another book crossed my path.
- Tracts kept showing up at work and I read them in the bathroom.
- I watched a televangelist and called the toll-free number on the screen.
- I had a dream or a vision.
- Other?

But what if one hasn't come to know Him yet? In your cancer battle, or that of your loved one, that is one's greatest need. Not only do I believe it's important, but God does. Why? Because cancer can be a matter of life and death. But there is life after death according to the Bible. Where will you spend eternity? God sent His only begotten son to earth that you might know Him.

Read John 3:16. Then please write it here.

_____

_____

_____

You've just handwritten your own invitation. Will you receive Him and His free gift of eternal life now? And do you want to know how to share Him with a loved one facing cancer? In the Bible, the New Testament Book of Romans outlines God's plan of salvation in its entirety. Please find the following Scriptures. In my Bible I've numbered them (1)-(5):

(1) Romans 3:23: "…for all have sinned and fall short of the glory of God."
(2) Romans 6:23: "For the wages of sin is death, but the free gift of God is eternal life in Christ Jesus our Lord."
(3) Romans 5:8: "But God demonstrates His own love toward us, in that while we were yet sinners, Christ died for us."
(4) Romans 10:13: "…for whoever will call upon the name of the Lord will be saved."
(5) Romans 10:9-10: "…if you confess with your mouth Jesus as Lord, and believe in your heart that God raised Him from the dead, you shall be saved; for with the heart a man believes, resulting in righteousness, and with the mouth he confesses, resulting in salvation."

Please pray, or ask your loved one to pray, this simple prayer with me:

Lord Jesus, I acknowledge before You that I am a sinner. I believe that You, Jesus, paid the wages for my sins, death, by Your death on the cross for me. I ask You to come into my heart now as Lord and Savior. I, by faith, receive You now and your free gift of eternal life.

Welcome to God's family and all the gifts and promises that follow. Salvation is an entry point, a doorway, and you may have heard the adage, "Don't stand in a doorway." So, let's continue our journey.

As I said in the first paragraph of *His Purpose*, our love and service will flow proportional to the height and breadth and depth of our knowledge of Him. Scripture is a treasure chest. As we read and study the Word we will grow in that knowledge. One way to study the Word is to explore the names of God: Father, Son, and Holy Spirit. Each reveals an aspect of His character. And there are at least 236 names found in Scripture. In Biblical times, a name was carefully chosen to identify a particular trait or characteristic and, if God-revealed, a prophetic sign of destiny and call, as John the Baptist (Luke 1:5-17) and Jesus (Luke 1:26-33). And a change of name was equally significant: Genesis 17:1-6, Abram (exalted father) to Abraham (father of many); 17:15 Sarai (princess) to Sarah (The Princess); Genesis 32:24-28, Jacob (supplanter) to Israel (a prince before God).

In our study of the 13 "P"s we will look at some of these revealed names of God. Let's start with the name *Jesus*. What does it mean?

_____

_____

*Jesus* is the Greek form of Joshua which means *the Lord saves*. The word *saved* from the Greek is *sozo* which will be covered in the next "P," *His Preparation*, and in the final chapter on prayer, where we will be reminded and admonished *to pray in the name of Jesus*.

Scripture Memory Verse:

"…but the people that do know their God shall be strong, and do exploits" Daniel 11:3 (KJV).

My Prayer for You:

That as you grow in the knowledge of God, you and your loved one(s) shall be strong and do valiantly in your cancer battle.

# CHAPTER TWO

---

## The second "P" is for *His Preparation.*

Psalm 10:17 (NKJV):
"Lord, You have heard the desire of the humble; You will prepare their heart…"

---

Does God prepare us for the circumstances ahead that we will need His grace to walk through? My experience suggests He does.

*My Story*

In 2014, as an inactive registered nurse, I applied to Medical Discipleship Training School, Youth With A Mission (YWAM), in Kona, Hawaii. I was accepted. Not unreasonable, as a nurse. But Youth With A Mission? I was seventy-two. I'm sure you're thinking, and rightly so, *God must have a sense of humor.* I think he does.

The base school lasted three months, and the foundation was laid for service outreach to the nations for the next eight weeks. As we prayed, one door that seemed open was Kurdistan, Iraq, ministering in a refugee camp of 30,000. My fear of going into this conflict-ridden geographic area bowed to the revelation that this was the cradle of civilization, the very probable site of Eden. But this door eventually closed and we were asked to pray about other options including Cambodia, though in the rainy season.

As I sought the Lord, I had a distinct impression He was quietly whispering in my spirit, 'I want to talk with you about your health. Your health is not good.' I only had one question, 'What should I do about it?' The answer came, 'Not go on outreach.' *Not go on outreach?* It seems I'd been preparing for thirty years, when I first wrote my testimony using these same 'P' words about 'Going,' going 'into the harvest field' (Matthew 28:18). First, I reviewed the steps I had been taught at YWAM before entering into petition. Had I followed them? Yes. I then rebuked the devil. But was this God? The thing that troubled me the most was that there had been a quiet weeping in my spirit following this disclosure. Was the Holy Spirit grieved or grieving? An ominous portent of what lie ahead?

Next, I shared this experience of my prayer time with the medical doctor leading outreach, Dr. Bob Doe. We met over lunch in the bustling outdoor arboretum/aviary-like cafeteria, the Pacific Ocean to the West, and mountains wrapping around the Eastern horizon, a breathtaking view. He thought there might be another door the Lord was indicating, possibly stateside, an Indian reservation in upstate New York, and the pastor from there would be on campus that very next week. But because of my one symptom, shortness of breath on exertion, he also scheduled a physical exam in the YWAM outreach clinic, Aloha Kona Urgent Care.

On exam, following a puzzling normal cardiogram, he proceeded with a full physical. A large abdominal mass was palpated. Lab studies followed, blood work and a CT scan. In case the mass was benign, I was asked if I'd still want to go on outreach. The answer came to my lips automatically, '*Yes.*'

The report came back suggestive of liposarcoma, a fatty cancerous tumor. Return to the mainland was advised. I'd be allowed to finish Discipleship Training School two short weeks away. But at this time the outreach would not be considered. I was then prompted by YWAM medical staff to schedule from Kona my follow-up on the mainland as time was of the essence. I was getting the impression that this was serious business. More to follow.

*Your Story*

In your cancer diagnosis or that of a loved one, can you see God's fingerprints of preparation? If so, how?

_____

_____

_____

_____

_____

_____

_____

_____

Perhaps you answered:

- Medical insurance through a job or spouse.
- Family home for the holidays just at that right time.
- The doctors optimistic report: "Caught it early…no lymph node involvement."
- Lived near a cancer center.
- If out of area, travel or housing provided by facility, family, or friends?

But these are necessary medical and/or surgical preparation involving the body. If man, as I believe, is a tripartite being, body, soul, and spirit, how can our spirit be prepared further for our or a loved one's cancer battle?

Let me tell you how the Lord prepared me. We studied in *His Purpose*, first and foremost by salvation. From the Greek, the word is *sozo*[1] meaning *safe: deliver or protect, heal, preserve, save (self), do well, be (make) whole*. The most commonly understood definition of *sozo* is *saved, salvation* as in Romans 10:9: "...if you confess with your mouth Jesus as Lord, and believe in your heart that God raised Him from the dead, you shall be saved..." The word here is *wholeness of the spirit*.

An example of *sozo* as *material and temporal deliverance from danger, suffering* is found in Luke 8:36: "...They also who had seen told them by what means he who had been demon-possessed was healed" (NKJV). This is *wholeness of the soul*.

Another usage of *sozo* is in Mark 5:24-29:

> ...a large crowd followed, pressing all around him. Among them was a woman who had had a hemorrhage for twelve years and had suffered a great deal under many physicians. She had spent her life savings; yet instead of improving, she had grown worse. She had heard about Yeshua, so she came up behind him in the crowd and touched his robe; for she said, 'If I touch even his clothes, I will be healed.' Instantly the hemorrhaging stopped, and she felt in her body that she had been healed from the disease...(CJB).

This is an example of *wholeness of the body*.

God's plan of salvation has more in store for the believer than life insurance (life assurance, eternal life) or fire insurance (saved from hell), but a complete wholeness, body, soul, and spirit and restoration to same.

Even in the natural, the World Health Organization defines health as "a state of complete physical, mental, and social well-being and not merely the absence of disease or infirmity." But God's definition adds the spiritual: "...Beloved, I pray that you may prosper in all things and be in health, just as your soul prospers" (3 John 2, NKJV). I love this verse. My prayer for you is that you "BE IN HEALTH."

*****

Another way the Lord has prepared me, and wants to prepare you, is found in a question the apostle Paul has for us.

Acts 19:1-6:

> It happened that while Apollos was at Corinth, Paul passed through the upper country and came to Ephesus, and found some disciples. He said to them, 'Did you receive the Holy Spirit when you believed?' And they said to him, 'No, we have not even heard whether there is a Holy Spirit.' And he said, 'Into what then were you baptized?' And they said, 'Into John's baptism.' Paul said, 'John baptized with the baptism of repentance, telling the people to believe in Him who was coming after him, that is, in Jesus.' When they heard this, they were baptized in the name of the Lord Jesus. And when Paul had laid his hands upon them, the Holy Spirit came on them, and they began speaking with tongues and prophesying.

Have you received the fullness of the Holy Spirit, as evidenced by speaking in tongues?

I believe Paul's question to believers was not doctrinal. 1 Corinthians 1:10-13 says:

> I appeal to you, dear brothers and sisters, by the authority of our Lord Jesus Christ, to live in harmony with each other. Let there be no divisions in the church. Rather, be of one mind, united in thought and purpose. For some members of Chloe's household have told me about your quarrels, my dear brothers and sisters. Some of you are saying, 'I am a follower of Paul.' Others are saying, 'I follow Apollos,' or 'I follow Peter,' or 'I follow only Christ.' Has Christ been divided into factions? (New Living Translation).

Paul's fervor for the fullness of the Holy Spirit as evidenced by speaking in tongues is recorded in 1 Corinthians 14:18: "I thank God, I speak in tongues more than you all…" I believe his reason was experiential. In Acts 13:9, Paul was formerly known as Saul. Look at the passages describing what happened at Ananias' laying on of hands in Acts 9:17-19:

> …Ananias…placed his hands on blind Saul, and said, 'Brother Saul, the Master sent me, the same Jesus you saw on your way here. He sent me so you could see again and be filled with the Holy Spirit.' No sooner were the words out of his mouth than something like scales fell from Saul's eyes—he could see again! He got to his feet, was baptized, and sat down with them to a hearty meal (The Message).

Blind! Now he could see! No wonder his enthusiasm for this experience of the manifestation of the Holy Spirit. Believer, do you yet see the connection? Healing!

Look at 1 Corinthians 12:4-11 and list the nine gifts of the Holy Spirit:

_____

_____

_____

_____

_____

_____

_____

_____

And Galatians 5:22-23, the nine fruits of the Holy Spirit:

_____

_____

_____

_____

_____

_____

_____

_____

The gift of the Holy Spirit ushers in the gifts and fruits that call us into our destiny and develop and empower our purpose.

And if we should need more evidence, science has contrasted praying with our spirit to praying with His:

> Dr. Andrew Newberg compared brain scans of Christians praying in tongues, Buddhist monks chanting during Meditation, and Catholic nuns praying. The study showed quite different results between those praying in tongues and the others. The frontal lobes—the part of the brain right behind the forehead that is considered the brain's control center—went quiet in the brains of the Christians talking in tongues. As the nuns prayed and the monks chanted, that part of their brains became more active. The discovery that Christians' frontal lobes go neutral while they are speaking in tongues proves that speaking in tongues is not a function of the natural brain, but an operation of the spirit.
>
> 'If I pray in a 'tongue' my spirit is praying, but my mind is inactive' (1 Corinthians 14:2, 14, PNT).[2]

But above all, the main reason for seeking the Holy Spirit should not be power or gifts, but Person: a relationship with Him, the third person of the Trinity, the Godhead, a treasure for those who find Him.

2 Corinthians 13:14: "I pray that you will enjoy the grace of the Lord Jesus Christ, the love of God, and the fellowship[3] of the Holy Spirit" (ERV).

Luke 11:13: "If you then, being evil, know how to give good gifts to your children, how much more will your heavenly Father give the Holy Spirit to those who ask Him?"

"*Seek the Giver, not the gift,*" words of wisdom from a leader in my church, then experiencing a world-wide outpouring of power and gifts. Stunned by this seeming rebuke that felt like a slap across the face, I didn't know then how much difference there is between the Giver and the Gift. I wanted power, absent from my life and would-be ministry, and the giftings that would usher that in. But His Presence...Oh, His Presence is the greatest gift of all. I call out His name, "Holy Spirit, come," and wait. He comes. When He comes, I know it before I know it, as soft, gentle tears begin to flow spontaneously from a well deep within. A hush comes over my spirit. I am in awe. All I can do is worship. He's here. He's actually here. I experience a love like I have never known, a love I need as much as oxygen. Beloved, I, no, more than I, He, wants that experience for you, too. How much more we need His Presence during and post-cancer treatment.

"…the love of God has been poured into our hearts by the Holy Spirit who has been given to us" (Romans 5:5, KJV).

Please pray and ask the Spirit of Truth, the Holy Spirit, to open the following Scriptures to you and reveal His truth from your favorite version of the Bible.

Summarize Matthew 3:13-17:

_____

_____

_____

_____

And Mark 16:17-18:

_____

_____

_____

And John 1:32-34:

_____

_____

_____

Acts 1:8:

_____

_____

_____

Acts 2:1-4:

_____

_____

_____

Acts 2:14-21:

_____

_____

_____

_____

_____

Hebrews 13:8:

_____

_____

Romans 5:5: "...we can't round up enough containers to hold everything God generously pours into our lives through the Holy Spirit!" (The Message).

Jesus Himself said in John 14:16-17:

> "I will ask the Father, and He will give you another Helper, that He may be with you forever; that is the Spirit of truth, whom the world cannot receive, because it does not see Him or know Him, but you know Him because He abides with you and will be in you."

And in John 16:7:

> "Let me assure you, it is better for you that I go away. I say this because when I go away I will send the Helper to you. But if I did not go, the Helper would not come" (ERV).

Which names of the Holy Spirit do you find in John 14:16-17 and John 16:7 above? Underline them, then compare how they read in your favorite translation.

The Holy Spirit is God. God prepared me for my cancer battle by His free gift of the Holy Spirit, His empowerment from heaven (Acts 1:8) to indwell me forever. Jesus Himself has asked the Father for this gift for you (John 14:16-17). Will you receive Him now? You only have to ask:

Come Holy Spirit, come. Jesus said if I asked in His name You would come. I invite You Holy Spirit. In Jesus name, I ask You now to come. Come with your wind. Come with your fire. I receive You now. Make me your tabernacle, your dwelling place forever.

*****

My preparation continued.

### My Story

In 2014, as I stood in my condo front doorway looking out, the thought *Vacation Bible School,* was forming. It was already late August. Yes, there were children here, even nearby neighbors. But in August? It took a village to execute a successful school, like the ones the American Bible Society prepared materials for, or those my children had attended past summers, religiously. But the thought was seeded in my spirit. Maybe it *was* the Lord's voice, but not the right timing? *Next year, Lord?* I queried. But *Vacation Bible School* kept naggingly recurring.

Even before a cancer diagnosis was made, I found myself struggling as to whether to go on outreach or not. My pay-as-I-go financial plan, monthly social security income, which I had presented to YWAM, was turned down. I was required to do a 'faith challenge' to raise support. Surprisingly, funding from church, family, and friends came easily and very quickly. The exact amount the school, YWAM University of the Nations, required for tuition, room and board was fully raised, but not a dime more. And the outstanding cost of outreach was possibly greater. The words *Vacation Bible School* still haunted me. Kona, Hawaii, walking distance from the Pacific Ocean, was my dream vacation, and I was fully immersed, eight hours a day, sometimes more, in the Word and discipleship training. And my pastor had shared before I left the church body, 'When it's God's will, He pays the bill.' But I did have social security income accruing these past three months…Was this Plan B?

In retrospect, I believe God's Plan A was only Medical Discipleship Training, my boot camp to become the warrior that God was preparing me to be in my cancer battle. And yes, *that* vacation bible school, adult version, my R and R before the war.

*****

How has God been preparing you? As food for thought let's look at another Bible story, about a shepherd boy God would anoint as king, and how God was preparing him to be "…a man after His own heart" (1 Samuel 13:14).

1 Samuel 17:34-37:

> But David said to Saul, 'Your servant was tending his father's sheep. When a lion or a bear came and took a lamb from the flock, I went out after him and attacked him, and rescued it from his mouth; and when he rose up against me, I seized him by his beard and struck him and killed him. Your servant has killed both the lion and the bear; and this uncircumcised Philistine will be like one of them, since he has taunted the armies of the living God.' And David said, 'The Lord who delivered me from the paw of the lion and from the paw of the bear, He will deliver me from the hand of this Philistine.'

This unnamed Philistine was the renowned giant Goliath who challenged the Israeli army to choose one man to fight against him. David, probably a teenager, had been sent by his father to carry lunch to his three elder brothers on the battlefront and bring back a report of their welfare. When he drew near the scene, he could hear the taunts of this giant. But no one dared answer his challenge. No one...but David. God had indeed prepared him. His history, though not on the battlefield, had conquered the bear and the lion. His weapons were not the king's sword nor armor, but a slingshot and five smooth stones. And he was anointed (1 Samuel 16:13).

What was your bear or your lion? What do you have in your battle armory? Five smooth stones, a sling shot tried and tested: life-line Scriptures from past battles that have prepared you for this present one?

_____

_____

_____

_____

David was not cloaked in the king's armor, but God's.

The Armor of God

Ephesians 6:10-18:

> Finally, be strong in the Lord and in the strength of His might. Put on the full armor of God, so that you will be able to stand firm against the schemes of the devil. For our struggle is not against flesh and blood, but against the rulers, against the powers, against the world forces of this darkness, against the spiritual forces of wickedness in the heavenly places. Therefore, take up the full armor of God, so that you will be able to resist in the evil day, and having done everything, to stand firm. Stand firm therefore, HAVING GIRDED YOUR LOINS WITH TRUTH, and HAVING PUT ON THE BREASTPLATE OF RIGHTEOUSNESS, and having shod YOUR FEET WITH THE PREPARATION OF THE GOSPEL OF PEACE; in addition to all, taking up the shield of faith with which you will be able to extinguish all the flaming arrows of the evil one. And take The HELMET OF SALVATION, and the sword of the Spirit, which is the word of God. With all prayer and petition pray at all times in the spirit...

The sword of the spirit is the Word of God. Let your smooth stones be Scriptures, tried and tested in battle, as you go forth against the giant, cancer, on behalf of yourself, patient/congregant, or a loved one.

Hebrews 4:12-13: "For the word of God is living and powerful, and sharper than any two-edged sword, piercing even to the division of soul and spirit, and of joints and marrow, and is a discerner of the thoughts and intents of the heart" (NKJV).

David declared the names of God over the giant, Goliath.

Each of the names of God was revealed and used in specific situations that confronted the believer. Each spoke of a unique aspect of *His character* that could provide the solution. For example, when little David faced huge Goliath, he proclaimed, 'You come to me with a sword, a spear, and a javelin, but I come to you in the name of the Lord of Hosts, the God of the armies of Israel, whom you have taunted' (1 Samuel 17:45). The 'Lord of Hosts' reveals He is commander of the hordes of angelic warriors, and 'God of the armies of Israel' means He is the omnipotent sovereign fighting for His people. How could Goliath possibly win against those odds?[4]

*My Story*

Go back in time with me, please, to 2004, the beautiful month of July. I am finishing a week-long on-site job as a clinical data abstractor in Laurinburg, NC, working for a Medicare-Medicaid Peer Review Organization. It has been a stressful week, as some charts were eighteen inches thick. For Quality Assurance, I am required to match my co-abstractor, even myself, on second selected charts. She finishes first. I lag behind, a nagging headache surfacing. Wanting to nip the pain in the bud, I stop for a caffeine fix at the nearest gas station.

Half-way home, the headache now worsened with nausea. I pull over at a familiar point to rest. I am not yet alarmed, due to my history of classic migraines. That evening it continues to worsen. I ask a friend to come over to be with me. In the back of my mind, I fear a trip to the ER. At 1 a.m. we make that trip.

The triage nurse checks my blood pressure. It is off the charts. So, a series of tests were ordered: EKG, portable chest, and kidney function. All come back normal. I am sent home in the care of a registered nurse, me, with instructions to return if my blood pressure continues to elevate.

I make it through the remainder of that day, but just as the next dawns, I call EMS. They find me nauseous with blood pressure off the charts again. I ride the ambulance this time.

The only system remaining to be checked from yesterday's workup is a CT of the head. It is promptly ordered and effected. The same resident that saw me the day before is working. As he enters my ER cubicle, his familiar face initially comforting, is now wearing a somber expression. 'We found your problem…a tumor on the brain. You've got to go for an MRI as soon as possible.'

The following week, I, with my son Jonathan, sit across from a neurosurgeon, reviewing lighted backdrop slices of my brain. He begins:

'It's probably a meningioma. Measures 2.5 centimeters, approximately one inch in diameter. It's located between the bony skull and the meninges, the lining of the brain. With no place to grow, it can cause pressure, median shift, edema, seizures or bleeding.

Probably a benign tumor. But it's too vascular an area to biopsy. Looking at his calendar then, he proceeds, 'Let's get this thing out. I can schedule you for surgery in the next two weeks.'

Waiting for my response, he looks up at me. I reply with a grin, 'There's only one problem. I checked *my* Day-Timer and I can't find brain surgery anywhere.'

When I sought the Lord for His battle plan then, I only heard one word, "Fight." That, dear reader, was July, 2004. Fast forward to July, 2021—that was seventeen years. I have not had brain surgery. The last MRI shows the tumor stable. MRI follow-up, once annual, has been discontinued. That battle has been, like David's, my bear, and my lion, preparing me for this one.

Scripture Memory Verse:

(Cancer) "You come to me with a sword, a spear, and a javelin, but I come to you in the name of The Lord of Hosts, the God of the armies of Israel, whom you have taunted" (1 Samuel 17:45).

My Prayer for You:

Lord of Hosts, God of the armies of Israel, this cancer, appearing to be a giant, is just an uncircumcised Philistine that taunts and defies You. Let a warrior spirit arise in you that you may put this enemy to flight. May you know "…the battle is the Lord's…" (1 Samuel 17:47).

# CHAPTER THREE

---

## The third "P" is for *His Plan.*

Matthew 28:18-20 (The Message):
"God authorized and commanded me to commission you: Go out and train everyone you meet, far and near, in this way of life, marking them by baptism in the threefold name: Father, Son, and Holy Spirit. Then instruct them in the practice of all I have commanded you. I'll be with you as you do this, day after day after day, right up to the end of the age."

---

I read here of a plan, both a mission, and a co-mission. We co-labor, since Pentecost, with the Holy Spirit to fulfill this Great Commission, to go and make disciples. But how can going into cancer treatment yourself or with a loved one be "going" as per Matthew 28:18?

*My Story*

The doctor who found the cancerous tumor was sending me back to the mainland for treatment. The tumor was large, estimated the size of three cucumbers and retro-peritoneal, thus possibly positioned inaccessible for surgery. He had not expressed any prognosis, favorable or otherwise. His silence hung in the very air, broken only by words I will never forget, 'You are going on outreach.'

*Your Story*

Yes, God has a plan. God has a (wo)man. That (wo)man is me/you. If I could not go to the nations, at Mayo Clinic the nations would come to me in the ethnic diversity of the medical staff and patients from around the globe. My "outreach" was not one I, or likely you, would have chosen.

In Genesis 6:14, the story of Noah, look at God's directive:

_____

_____

The God who created the heavens and the earth, an entire universe, in six days surely could have spoken a mere boat into existence. But He commissioned Noah to co-labor with Him in building the ark that would save (*sozo*) his family from the flood that was to come, ravishing the earth and destroying every other living thing. Two character traits of Jehovah are revealed in this story: a covenant making/keeping God and a God who remembers. Apply these in your cancer battle.

See Genesis 6:18:

_____

_____

Genesis 8:1:

_____

_____

Summarize Genesis 9:9-17:

_____

_____

_____

_____

And look at the Old Testament story of Jonah's call to Nineveh. Was this a place Jonah asked or wanted to go? See Jonah 1:1-3. Paraphrase this encounter.

_____

_____

_____

What was the result of Jonah's actions? See Jonah 1:4-17.

_____

_____

_____

_____

In Jonah 2:1, Jonah has a change of mind and heart. Describe this from versus 1-10.

_____

_____

In Jonah 3:1-3, the word of the Lord comes to Jonah again. Was the word different or was Jonah's response?

_____

_____

What was the result of Jonah's obedience? See Jonah 3:4-10.

_____

_____

In Chapter 4, versus 1-3, what was Jonah's reaction?

_____

_____

_____

In Chapter 4:4-8, God gives Jonah a "show and tell," an object lesson. What was it?

_____

_____

_____

Jonah is still angry, even more so than previously. How does God rebuke him in versus 9-11?

_____

_____

_____

The result of Jonah's going was salvation for a city. Also, look at the story of Esther (Esther 2:7-9:32), an orphan, who left Mordecai, her adoptive home, to enter a harem. Could God be in this? Yes, salvation resulted for the Jewish nation. Or consider Joseph (Genesis 37), like Jesus being carried by another Joseph (Matthew 2:13-15) down to Egypt. Could good come out of these flights? Yes, both were deliverers. The former accomplished salvation from famine for a family, a tribe, a nation, and the latter, Jesus, salvation from eternal damnation by His death on a cross at Calvary for all of mankind who call on His name.

Allow God to partner with you in your cancer journey. What will your "going" accomplish as you co-labor with Him?

Look at Matthew 28:18, 20: "…Go…I'll be with you as you do this, day after day after day, right up to the end of the age." When we go through the door set before us, God's Holy Spirit will go with us. We have only to invite Him into our heart and life. Our "going" where God leads us, too, can be a fulfilling of the Great Commission (Mathew 28:18-20) making disciples. It's a daily choice. In 2 Corinthians 3:2-3 Paul writes:

> "You yourselves are our letter of recommendation, written on our hearts, known and read by everyone. You make it clear that you are a letter from the Messiah placed in our care, written not with ink but by the Spirit of the living God, not on stone tablets but on human hearts" (CJB).

As part of our "going," we may have to forgive those who have hurt us, or who we've hurt, reconciling some relationships along the way. Healing of body, soul, and spirit is a process, an on-going process. And one of the obstacles to healing is unforgiveness, as it hinders our prayers (Matthew 6:12).

Those who read the book of our lives, our children and families, co-workers, friends and acquaintances, can also, if they seek, find Him who saves from hell, sickness of body, soul, and spirit. As you go, take others along with you. This is God's plan for you. And it's a good plan.

Look up Jeremiah 29:11 in your favorite Bible translation. This is your Scripture memory verse and my prayer for you:

_____

_____

_____

_____

If you have accepted Jesus as Savior, have you made Him Lord of your life? Of the different names of God, *Jehovah* or *Lord*, is used 6,823 times in the Old Testament, and speaks of God's being or essence.[1] When a hyphen follows, an additional characteristic of His nature, His character, is revealed. In subsequent chapters we will study some of these compound names, including *Jehovah-jireh* (*The Lord will provide*), *Jehovah-shalom* (*The Lord is Peace*), and *Jehovah-rapha* (*The Lord that heals*). Do you know Him yet as Lord?

Please stop here now and invite Him to reveal Himself as *Jehovah, Lord*. As you grow in knowledge of Him, ask Him to be Lord of your life if you have not already done so. Write out and date your prayer here as a reminder of this life-altering action.

_____

_____

_____

_____

# CHAPTER FOUR

---

## The fourth "P" is for *His Provision.*

Genesis 22:14:
"Abraham called the name of that place The Lord Will Provide, as it is said to
this day, 'In the mount of the Lord, it will be provided.'"

---

*My Story* left off in Kona, continues…
From my journal…June 28, 2015:

KOA (Kona International Airport) to LAX, (Los Angeles International Airport),
United Airlines, 37,000 feet:

I had left a gift, an inflatable flight pillow, in my YWAM dorm room with a note:
'For whosoever will…' (claim it). As I thought about this from my aisle seat, the words
were Scriptural: 'Whoever will…call upon the name of the Lord, will be saved' (Romans
10:13). Saved? From what? Cancer?

I remembered then a story that my mother had told me long ago. She was standing
in our kitchen in front of a picture of Jesus, light rays emanating from His heart. She
was praying, palms upturned, herself her morning offering, when the wire holding the
picture suddenly broke and she was able in this posture to catch the picture in mid-air.
Later that day she would learn that my father, an exterior house painter, was on a scaffold
at that very moment, when the rope broke. He was able to catch the other end, stopping
his fall to the ground far below.

With this in mind, I then offered the sacrifice of my life to God again. I had done
this in the YWAM Chapel the night I was dropped off on campus from Aloha Urgent
Care, diagnosis revealed. I had laid the paperwork, my printed MRI scan and lab results,
on that altar. And symbolically, the presumptive cancer cells. But in exchange for what?
My life? No, His. His life. Isaiah came to mind. His stripes. '…And by His stripes we
are healed' (Isaiah 53:5, NKJV). His stripes for my healing. Cool tears came not from
sadness, but from the very Presence of God. Cool refreshing water of the Holy Spirit.

*Your Story*

"The Lord will provide" in Hebrew, is *Jehovah-jireh* (Genesis 22:14). Let's look at this entire story now:

Genesis 22:1-4:

> God tested Abraham, and said to him, 'Abraham!' And he said, 'Here I am.' He said, 'Take now your son, your only son, whom you love, Isaac, and go to the land of Moriah, and offer him there as a burnt offering on one of the mountains of which I will tell you.' So Abraham rose early in the morning and saddled his donkey, and took two of his young men with him and Isaac his son; and he split wood for the burnt offering, and arose and went to the place of which God had told him. On the third day Abraham raised his eyes and saw the place from a distance.

Where was Abraham told to go?

_____

What was he asked to do when he got there?

_____

_____

Look at Genesis 22:1. God is said here to have "tested" Abraham. What prior encounters with God could have possibly prepared him for this test? How could he be sure that it was "God," God's voice?

_____

_____

_____

_____

Did you remember and answer:

• God's call to Abraham from Ur of the Chaldeans, leaving kinsman?
• God's covenant promise that Abraham's descendants would be as numerous as the stars of heaven?
• Or God's prophecy/promise at his tent that Sarai in her old age would bear Abraham a son?

Abraham had come to know God's voice. He had learned faith and God's faithfulness. Have you? If so, where?

_____

_____

Look back over Abraham's story on Mount Moriah. Is sacrifice the ending?

Genesis 22:7-8: "Isaac spoke to Abraham his father and said, 'My father!' And he said, 'Here I am, my son.' And he said, 'Behold, the fire and the wood, but where is the lamb for the burnt offering?' Abraham said, 'God will provide for Himself the lamb for the burnt offering, my son.' So the two of them walked on together."

Do you see the faith declaration here? And earlier in Genesis 22:5:

"Abraham said to his young men, 'Stay here with the donkey, and I and the lad will go over there; and we will worship and return to you.'"

The story continues with Genesis 22:9-14:

Then they came to the place of which God had told him; and Abraham built the altar there and arranged the wood, and bound his son Isaac and laid him on the altar, on top of the wood. Abraham stretched out his hand and took the knife to slay his son. But the angel of the Lord called to him from heaven and said, 'Abraham, Abraham!' And he said, 'Here I am.' He said, 'Do not stretch out your hand against the lad, and do nothing to him; for now I know that you fear God, since you have not withheld your son, your only son, from Me.' Then Abraham raised his eyes and looked, and behold, behind him a ram caught in the thicket by his horns; and Abraham went and took the ram and offered him up for a burnt offering in the place of his son. Abraham called the name of that place The Lord Will Provide, as it is said to this day, 'In the mount of the Lord it will be provided.'

The story of Abraham and Isaac ends not with sacrifice, but provision. *Jehovah-jireh*: *On the mountain of the Lord, it will be provided.* Did God's call to "go" take Abraham to a place he didn't want to go? Will yours and mine? Possibly. Remember Jonah's call to Nineveh (Jonah 1:1-3), Esther's call to enter a harem (Esther 2:7-9:32), and Joseph's and Jesus' flight into Egypt (Genesis 37, Matthew 2:13-14)? Your first "going" needs to be "going" to God. He is a holy mountain. In Him, you will find all the provision you will ever need. Then present your whole self a living sacrifice to Him.

Romans 12:1: "So I beg you, brothers and sisters, because of the great mercy God has shown us, offer your lives as a living sacrifice to him—an offering that is only for God and pleasing to him" (ERV).

Will your provision, like Abraham's, come after you offer your gift, yourself, at the altar? I needed healing however God would provide that…if through doctors, then the right cancer center, housing, and family support. God provided these.

## *My Story*

From Kona, I was coming back only to a car and a storage unit in Surfside Beach, SC. I had not been able to find a roommate for my beach apartment to share expenses for the months I would be gone. So, had given notice to vacate my unit, having put everything in storage. I had a housing offer from a YWAM sister to come to Minnesota, Mayo Clinic Main campus. From there she offered to drive me round trip for whatever my treatment would require. I hardly knew her. She had followed the diagnostic process through intercession and we often sat together in the Kona cafeteria. Minnesota would be cold. All my winter clothes, if accessible, were in the back of my storage unit. But mentally I saw myself packing to go there. When my son David in Gainesville, at the University of Florida, heard my plan, he counter-offered. He was graduating, and giving up his apartment soon also, but he offered to see me through my treatment in its entirety. Wow! There was a cancer center in Gainesville at the University, and I tried to make an on-line application for an appointment from Kona. But I lost the internet site and Mayo Clinic kept popping up. And there was a Mayo Clinic site in Jacksonville, Florida, ninety minutes away from David. I made an appointment with my primary care physician in Surfside Beach before arrival, and hand-carried the Mayo physician's referral form I had downloaded. The very next day I had a telephone call from an oncologist specializing in sarcoma, the diagnosis my Kona doctor had made, and an appointment a few days away. David would drive to Surfside where I was staying in a motel, leave my car behind again, and then drive together to Gainesville.

## *Your Story*

What do you or your loved one need God to provide at this very time in your life? Or in retrospect, how has God already provided?

_____

_____

_____

_____

_____

_____

_____

Test Yourself
God's name, *Jehovah-jireh,* means:

_____

_____

Scripture Memory Verse and My Prayer for You:

Philippians 4:19-20:
"And my God will supply all your needs according to His riches in glory in Christ Jesus.
Now to our God and Father be the glory forever and ever. Amen."

# CHAPTER FIVE

---

## The fifth "P" is for *His Peace.*

Judges 6:23:
"Peace to you, do not fear; you shall not die."

---

Has a cancer diagnosis disturbed your peace or that of a loved one? Has it opened up for you a seeming Pandora's Box of fear? If you would honestly name those fears, what would they be?

- Fear of _____
- Fear of _____
- Fear of _____
- Fear of _____
- Fear of _____
- Fear of _____
- Fear of _____

My son David's mother-in-law, Jen, was diagnosed with breast cancer just before Christmas. I read an internet post from her, grieving the potential loss of both breasts. But what struck me the most was her statement, "The battlefield is the mind...I wish I knew more Scripture." Yes, I agree. *The war on cancer is won, one battle at a time, one thought at a time.*

2 Corinthians 10:3-5: "For though we walk in the flesh, we do not war according to the flesh, for the weapons of our warfare are not of the flesh, but divinely powerful for the destruction of fortresses. We are destroying speculations and every lofty thing raised up against the knowledge of God, and we are taking every thought captive to the obedience of Christ..."

Isaiah 55:10-11:
For as the rain comes down, and the snow from heaven,
And do not return there,
But water the earth,
And make it bring forth and bud,
That it may give seed to the sower
And bread to the eater,
So shall My word be that goes forth from My mouth;
It shall not return to Me void,

But it shall accomplish what I please,
And it shall prosper in the thing for which I sent it (NKJV).

Our war on cancer begins with our very thoughts. Fear thoughts—whether fear of diagnosis, disease progression, treatment, death, pain, body image change, financial or physical disability or other (as you've filled in the blanks) must bow to the Lordship of Jesus Christ.

## *My Story*

Travel went well. Left at 5:30 a.m. for a 7:30 a.m. intake at Mayo Clinic with six minutes to spare! Met the medical oncologist, Dr. Attia, a University of Florida grad like David. He is knowledgeable, specializes in sarcoma, and has a team at his fingertips.

In honesty, when I saw my pics (CT), I cried, then made a bad joke, 'I don't like this 'selfie." The tumor appears humongous, and I must remember it is only a Goliath, an uncircumcised Philistine taunting the army (*me*) of the living God. But to see my right kidney enlarged and displaced mid-abdomen was surreal. First, Dr. A. is after what the tumor is, so a visualized ultrasound biopsy is scheduled ASAP, therefore tomorrow at high noon. An MRI of the abdomen and pelvis follows at 8:15 p.m., and I should return the next morning for CT of the chest and the follow-up results. I am on the fast track.

The proposed plan, if it is the suspected type of tumor: five weeks of radiation, a month cool-down, followed by surgery.

The only downside thus far is that Mayo doesn't accept Medicare consignment. I submit the bills directly. My copay is the standard 20%, and then Mayo charges a 15% differential. I could go elsewhere for radiation, but the surgeon is a master from Mayo Rochester and the radiologist who maps my treatment, the former head of radiology, Rochester, MN. I was asked by Dr. A., 'What is your life worth?' Food for thought and prayer. I learned in Medical Discipleship Training, Kona, 'I am precious and priceless and dearly loved by my Heavenly Father.'

Let's look again at Judges 6:23: "Peace to you, do not fear; you shall not die." In context, this is one verse of Judges 6:11-24, the story of Gideon, set in biblical times of great fear and oppression. If you can relate to verse 23, read the story in its entirety, Judges 6:11-24, reprinted at the end of this chapter, or in your favorite version.

Where was Gideon at the time of his visitation? (Judges 6:11)

_____

_____

What was he doing? (Judges 6:11)

_____

_____

What did the angel of the Lord say to him? (Judges 6:12)

_____

_____

What was Gideon's response? (Judges 6:13)

_____

_____

_____

What was the Lord's commission? (Judges 6:14)

_____

_____

_____

What was Gideon's initial response to this command to "Go…"? (Judges 6:15)

_____

_____

_____

Have you ever felt likewise? Is the diagnosis of cancer, in your own strength, an impossible challenge to meet?

_____

_____

_____

Does God leave Gideon there, abandoned to his resources, his strengths? Find the answer in Judges 6:16.

_____

_____

But does this settle the issue once and for all for Gideon? Read Judges 6:17-19.

_____

_____

_____

And what is God's intervention? (Judges 6:20-21)

_____

_____

Has obedience ever felt like it required a burnt offering of all your hopes, dreams, and expectations of even God's promises? Describe such a time, if you've known one in your or your loved one's cancer experience.

_____

_____

_____

_____

Compare from your favorite translation, Exodus 3:1-21, the call of another deliverer, Moses.

"Therefore, come now, and I will send you to Pharaoh, so that you may
bring My people, the sons of Israel, out of Egypt" (Exodus 3:10).

Where was Moses when the call of God came to him (Exodus 3:1), and how did he get there? (Exodus 2:11-22)

_____

_____

What was Moses' response? (Exodus 3:11, 4:10-13)

_____

_____

_____

What was God's response to Moses? (Exodus 4:14-17)

_____

_____

_____

Have you found reasons why going through cancer would be difficult? The timing inconvenient? Like Gideon, did you need or did you ask for a sign (Judges 6:36-40) or like Moses, did God give you one (Exodus 4:21)? Can you describe such a time in your or your loved one's cancer experience?

_____

_____

_____

_____

For me, Kubler-Ross' stages of grief come to mind: denial, anger, bargaining, depression, and acceptance. Can you relate to these? If you can, where at this moment are you in the grief process? And what specifically are you grieving?

_____

_____

For you, where is God in this process? Do you see or sense His direction? His intervention(s)?

_____

_____

My Prayer for You, your loved one, is you come to know, like Gideon, that *The Lord is Peace.* Your Scripture Memory Verses are Isaiah 53:5 and Isaiah 55:12-13.

Isaiah 53:5: "The chastisement for our peace was upon Him…" (NKJV).

Isaiah 55:12-13:
For you will go out with joy
And be led forth with peace;
The mountains and the hills will break forth into shouts of joy before you,
And all the trees of the field will clap their hands.
13 Instead of the thorn bush the cypress will come up,
And instead of the nettle the myrtle will come up,
And it will be a memorial to the Lord,
For an everlasting sign which will not be cut off.

Look for Him, His Peace, in your daily walk. Peace is a person, the Lord Jesus Christ. If you've received Him as Savior and Lord, you carry Him inside. You carry Him everywhere you go.

Test Yourself
God's name, *Jehovah-shalom,*[1] means?

_____

_____

Judges 6:11-24
Gideon Is Visited

Then the angel of the Lord came and sat under the oak that was in Ophrah, which belonged to Joash the Abiezrite as his son Gideon was beating out wheat in the wine press in order to save it from the Midianites. 12 The angel of the Lord appeared to him and said to him, 'The Lord is with you, O valiant warrior.' 13 Then Gideon said to him, 'O my lord, if the Lord is with us, why then has all this happened to us? And where are all His miracles which our fathers told us about, saying, 'Did not the Lord bring us up from Egypt?' But now the Lord has abandoned us and given us into the hand of Midian.' 14 The Lord looked at him and said, 'Go in this your strength and deliver Israel from the hand of Midian. Have I not sent you?' 15 He said to Him, 'O Lord, how shall I deliver Israel? Behold, my family is the least in Manasseh, and I am the youngest in my father's house.' 16 But the Lord said to him, 'Surely I will be with you, and you shall defeat Midian as one man.' 17 So Gideon said to Him, 'If now I have found favor in Your sight, then show me a sign that it is You who speak with me. 18 'Please do not depart from here, until I come back to You, and bring out my offering and lay it before You.' And He said, 'I will remain until you return.'

19 Then Gideon went in and prepared a young goat and unleavened bread from an ephah of flour; he put the meat in a basket and the broth in a pot, and brought them out to him under the oak and presented them. 20 The angel of God said to him, 'Take the

meat and the unleavened bread and lay them on this rock, and pour out the broth.' And he did so. 21 Then the angel of the Lord put out the end of the staff that was in his hand and touched the meat and the unleavened bread; and fire sprang up from the rock and consumed the meat and the unleavened bread. Then the angel of the Lord vanished from his sight. 22 When Gideon saw that he was the angel of the Lord, he said, 'Alas, O Lord God! For now I have seen the angel of the Lord face to face.' 23 The Lord said to him, 'Peace to you, do not fear; you shall not die.' 24 Then Gideon built an altar there to the Lord and named it The Lord is Peace. To this day it is still in Ophrah of the Abiezrites.

# CHAPTER SIX

---

## The sixth "P" is for *His Presence.*

John 10:3-4 (ESV):
"The sheep hear his voice, and he calls his own sheep by name and leads
them out. When he has brought out all his own, he goes before them,
and the sheep follow him, for they know his voice."

---

Yes, He goes before you. He goes with you. He leads the way, even through cancer. The name of God, *Jehovah-shammah*, means *The Lord is There*. It's His Presence with us in any place we find ourselves that makes all the difference. A pastor I know calls Psalm 139, "The Presence" Psalm. Here is an excerpt:

7 Where can I go from Your Spirit?
Or where can I flee from Your presence?
8 If I ascend to heaven, You are there;
9 If I take the wings of the dawn,
If I dwell in the remotest part of the sea,
10 Even there Your hand will lead me,
And Your right hand will lay hold of me.
11 If I say, 'Surely the darkness will overwhelm me,
And the light around me will be night,'
12 Even the darkness is not dark to You,
And the night is as bright as the day. Darkness and light are alike to You.

What does God promise will always, as born-again believers, go with us? John 10:4:

_____

_____

Where can we go apart from God's Presence (Psalm 139:7-12)?

_____

_____

As a child, were you ever afraid of the dark, feeling engulfed? As an adult, our darkness may be different: not seeing the next step to take, not knowing where the next resource will come from; or even the spiritual darkness, at a low point in our lives, of questioning where God is. Can you describe such a time as this in your cancer battle or that of your loved one?

_____

_____

_____

_____

What does Psalm 139:11-12 say about darkness?

_____

_____

Heaven? (Psalm 139:8)

_____

_____

The remotest part of the sea? (Psalm 139:9-10)

_____

_____

How can you or your loved one practice the Presence of God during your/their cancer treatment?

_____

_____

_____

*My Story*

The Lord seemed to be leading me, indeed. First, a cancer treatment center, temporary housing, and family support as described in the previous chapter. Now the treatment plan itself. There would be a team, an oncologist, a radiologist, a surgeon, nurses, and a medical social worker. But first, more tests, a biopsy of the tumor, repeated trips to Jacksonville over the next weeks, scans of the abdomen, pelvis, and lung to rule out metastasis, fittings in radiology to create a shield for organs not involved, and skin mapping marks for the radiation area itself. In one of my early appointments at Mayo Clinic, I learned about a housing option for out-of-area patients on the West campus of Mayo Clinic, Jacksonville, Gabriel House. But residency required the accompaniment of a caregiver, regardless of how self-sufficient one actually appeared. Once my treatment plan established that I would need twenty-five radiation treatments to my abdomen and pelvis, five days a week for five weeks, I knew I had to be closer.

In rush hour, the commute both to and from Gainesville could be three hours one way. My son David was resistive to the prospect of Gabriel House from the start, citing his uncomfortableness around people. As the date for the start of radiation treatment loomed closer, I asked him to just drive by there. We sat in the car outside together in silence and took in the mansion with its circular driveway, situated on a picturesque, wooded lake. Nothing more was said. But a change of mind and heart came over David. We applied and moved in the day of my first radiation treatment. Our room assignment on the first floor, which housed cancer patients, overlooked that very lake. It would be our home for the next five weeks.

In the library at Gabriel House, I found a book titled, *The Anatomy of Hope*, by Jerome Groopman, M.D. documenting a hopeless case: a Harvard professor, chair of the department of pathology, with a diagnosis of stomach cancer. In it, the patient says, 'I want to live, so I had to fight—the mustering of the will to engage the foe and the strength to sustain the battle, in themselves, became a form of victory—I recited the Twenty-third Psalm—before, during, and after each treatment. It spoke so beautifully, so directly, to my plight'[1] His outcome, against all odds, was life.

So, let's look at Psalm 23 now together, but personalizing it by putting your name in the blanks.

The Lord is _____ shepherd, _____ shall not want. He makes _____ lie down in green pastures; He leads _____ beside quiet waters. He restores _____ soul; He guides _____ in the paths of righteousness For His name's sake. Even though _____ walk through the valley of the shadow of death, _____ fear no evil, for You are with _____; Your rod and Your staff, they comfort _____. You prepare a table before _____ in the presence of _____ enemies; You have anointed _____ head with oil; _____ cup overflows. Surely goodness and lovingkindness will follow _____ all the days of ____ life, And _____ will dwell in the house of the Lord forever.

*My Story* continues…

Radiation treatment is harder and longer than I expected. David prays with me, hugs me, and then drops me off at the entrance, parks, then waits patiently for me in the adjoining waiting area. The promised 'four minutes of treatment, in and out in fifteen' has stretched to thirty, and now totals forty-five minutes on the cold slab table. I quickly run through the Twenty-third Psalm and seemingly every other Scripture verse I have committed to memory. The piped-in Christian music helps too. Because of the length of my treatments, the time slot shifts repeatedly for the one available room that can accommodate me. When I'm finished for another day, and I am counting down from twenty-five, my proposed treatment plan, we walk together to where David has found free campus parking. The ritual helps, as so much of my life is outside my control right now.

But the presence of God through David's tangible hug is so real; his prayer, the Father's words of love and care for me, and his visible waiting keeps God's invisible presence so close. Add to this a prophetic word from a sister in Christ who would be one of my on-going intercessors:

'God's power to radiate through the radiation and spread His glory into every cell of your body, pushing every cancer cell out and replacing them with healthy cells. By His stripes! Healing manifest, in Jesus' name.'

## Your Life Application

*The Practice of the Presence of God* comes to mind, the story of a monk who sought and experienced God's Presence in every simple daily activity, especially the routine and mundane, like washing dishes. Yes, I believe we, too, can develop a sensitivity to find God as we seek him throughout our day. Remember the children's puzzle maze of people, "Where's Waldo?" Apply that to God. Find God in your every day, every day. This is the best preparation to take Him when and wherever you go.

A pastor friend, reminiscent to me of the television-prompt, "It's eleven o'clock. Do you know where your children are?" sets his phone alarm to "check-in" with God at various points in his day. It's a private alert to find where his heart is and turn it God-ward.

Or we could leave a Bible open where we eat lunch, countertop, or in the car. Or carry a pocket New Testament or Scripture cards in a purse or wallet. I have created flash cards, 3 by 5 inch index cards with topical Scriptures that the Lord has quickened to me. As I wait in line at the checkout or drive-through, I read and memorize a verse or two to add to my storehouse.

And I try to remember to listen: I ask God questions, directions throughout the day, and then wait on Him to answer.

My favorite is from Bible teacher Beth Moore that she calls GodStop, the acronym STOP, *Savoring The Observable Presence.*

Part of our faith-walk experience will be learning to recognize God in our midst by noticing visible prints of His invisible hands. When God makes Himself observable we want to stop and take notice. I want to learn to say to myself, That's God! Stop and savor the moment! A Godstop is any means by which God seems to go out of His way during your day to make Himself known to you…any answered prayer…any occurrence that you know is more than a coincidence…meant for bedtime, based on Psalm 63:6: 'On my bed I remember you.' One of the greatest builders of our faith tomorrow is remembering ways He worked today.[2]

I date and record these in my faith journal, a converted gratitude journal allowing up to five entries per date.

In YWAM, I was required to do assigned weekly Scripture memory verses. And every Friday, we were tested, asked to write out the verse or verses. I found I could memorize best when I wrote the words repeatedly. It involves more senses. In YWAM, people memorized whole books of the Bible, chapter by chapter, one verse at a time. It was not uncommon to encounter someone anywhere—cafeteria, bathroom, walking—speaking Scripture aloud.

Your Scripture memory verses are Isaiah 8:10 and Psalm 91:1-2.

Isaiah 8:10: "Because when all is said and done, the last word is Immanuel—God-With-Us" (The Message).

My favorite, Psalm 91, and My Prayer for You, talks of the safety of abiding in the Presence of God: "He who dwells in the secret place of the Most High shall abide under the shadow of the Almighty" (NKJV).

Psalm 91:1-2:
You who sit down in the High God's presence,
spend the night in Shaddai's shadow,
2 Say this: 'God, you're my refuge.
I trust in you and I'm safe!'
(The Message).

If you come from a family background of addiction or abuse, you may have issues with fear of abandonment. These Presence Scriptures will replace the lies you may have believed as a child. Commit them to memory, so you are building a shelter, a hiding place for The Most High God within you that you can take with you, *before* you *"Go"* through darkness. Spend time there. And if darkness is already upon you, "Go" to the holy mountain that is your God, as Abraham did. Remember that darkness and light are alike to Him. (Psalm 139:12).

1 John 1:5: "…God is Light, and in Him there is no darkness at all."

Test Yourself
God's name, *Jehovah-shammah*, means

_____

_____

# CHAPTER SEVEN

---

## The seventh "P" is, for *His own, His Promises.*

2 Corinthians 1:20-21:
"For as many as are the promises of God, in Him they are yes; therefore also through Him is our Amen to the glory of God through us."

---

I have a worn, coverless pocket *Promise* book that lists 867 promises to me, as a believer, from the Word of God. Let's look at one Bible story that illustrates a promise of God through His prophet Elijah and His revelation of Himself as the Promise Keeper.

1 Kings 17:8-13:

Then the word of the Lord came to him, saying, 9 'Arise, go to Zarephath, which belongs to Sidon, and stay there; behold, I have commanded a widow there to provide for you.' 10 So he arose and went to Zarephath, and when he came to the gate of the city, behold, a widow was there gathering sticks; and he called to her and said, 'Please get me a little water in a jar, that I may drink.' 11 As she was going to get it, he called to her and said, 'Please bring me a piece of bread in your hand.' 12 But she said, 'As the Lord your God lives, I have no bread, only a handful of flour in the bowl and a little oil in the jar; and behold, I am gathering a few sticks that I may go in and prepare for me and my son, that we may eat it and die.' 13 Then Elijah said to her, 'Do not fear; go, do as you have said, but make me a little bread cake from it first and bring it out to me, and afterward you may make one for yourself and for your son.'

Has God ever asked you, it seemed, in your cancer battle to give more than you had to give, or perhaps were willing or able to give? Does anything come to mind?

_____

_____

_____

_____

But with the sacrifice is there a promise in His word, or a personal prophecy, that accompanied it?

_____

_____

_____

_____

For the widow of Zarephath there was in 1 Kings 17:14-16:

> For thus says the Lord God of Israel, 'The bowl of flour shall not be exhausted, nor shall the jar of oil be empty, until the day that the Lord sends rain on the face of the earth.' 15 So she went and did according to the word of Elijah, and she and he and her household ate for many days. 16 The bowl of flour was not exhausted nor did the jar of oil become empty, according to the word of the Lord which He spoke through Elijah.

By all accounts, this would be a happy ending. But does the widow's story as recorded end here?
1 Kings 17:17-18: "Now it came about after these things that the son of the woman, the mistress of the house, became sick; and his sickness was so severe that there was no breath left in him. 18 So she said to Elijah, 'What do I have to do with you, O man of God? You have come to me to bring my iniquity to remembrance and to put my son to death.'"

This new crisis overrides the previous one of famine. But God, through the prophet, is not finished with the widow's story. Or yours.

I Kings 17:19-24:

> He said to her, 'Give me your son.' Then he took him from her bosom and carried him up to the upper room where he was living, and laid him on his own bed. 20 He called to the Lord and said, 'O Lord my God, have You also brought calamity to the widow with whom I am staying, by causing her son to die?' 21 Then he stretched himself upon the child three times, and called to the Lord and said, 'O Lord my God, I pray You, let this child's life return to him.' 22 The Lord heard the voice of Elijah, and the life of the child returned to him and he revived. 23 Elijah took the child and brought him down from the upper room into the house and gave him to his mother; and Elijah said, 'See, your son is alive.' 24 Then the woman said to Elijah, 'Now I know that you are a man of God and that the word of the Lord in your mouth is truth.'

God wrote an even happier ending. What fragments of your story need to be rewritten? Where do you need God's intervention to make a happy ending to a chapter?

_____

_____

_____

_____

Remember that God isn't finished with you, or your story, yet. When you read your life story backward to the beginning, look for promises fulfilled, places where it was evident that the Lord met your need. He who is faithful, can only continue to be faithful. It is His very nature. And you, too, are called to be faithful, full of faith in His Word, His promises to you. Take them with you when you "Go" into and through your battle(s).

## Life Application

Look back over your life and journal those Scripture lifelines that you see, the places where God through His Word, or the word of prophecy, has met you in the past. And there, in the future, He will meet you again. It's a promise, like a blank check. Only you can fill in your name—and take it to the bank. But remember, and do not be discouraged, as in Scripture there is often a wilderness between the promise(s) and the promised land, your inheritance in Christ; and many in Scripture, as in life, "…died in faith, not having received the promises, but having seen them afar off were assured of them, embraced them and confessed that they were strangers and pilgrims on the earth…for He has prepared a city for them" (Hebrews 11:13,16, NKJV).

Is there is a particular area of your life where you, like me, are still waiting for the fulfillment of a word, a _rhema_[1]? Are there giants? Describe that here.

_____

_____

_____

_____

I encourage you to find and write out God's promises in that area, carry them on index cards, akin to flash cards. Memorize those promises. Meditate on them. Let them marinate until they become flesh, faith. Write your first one here as your Scripture memory verse for this chapter:

_____

_____

_____

_____

Or if you are new to finding God's promises in His Word, borrow one of my favorites:

Isaiah 43:2-3:
"When you pass through the waters, I will be with you;
and through the rivers, they shall not overwhelm you;
when you walk through fire you shall not be burned,
and the flame shall not consume you.
For I am the Lord your God, the Holy One of Israel, your Savior" (ESV).

Or borrow from Charles Spurgeon, the English Baptist preacher known as the "Prince of Preachers." Though he died in 1892 his words live on:

"Remember the word unto Thy servant, upon which Thou hast caused me to hope."
Psalm 119:49

Whatever your especial need may be, you may readily find some promise in the Bible suited to it. Are you faint and feeble because your way is rough and you are weary? Here is the promise—'He giveth power to the faint.' When you read such a promise, take it back to the great Promiser, and ask Him to fulfill His own word. Are you seeking after Christ, and thirsting for closer communion with Him? This promise shines like a star upon you—'Blessed are they that hunger and thirst after righteousness, for they shall be filled.' Take that promise to the throne continually; do not plead anything else, but go to God over and over again with this—'Lord, Thou hast said it, do as Thou hast said.' Are you distressed because of sin, and burdened with the heavy load of your iniquities? Listen to these words—'I, even I, am He that blotteth out thy transgressions, and will no more remember thy sins.' You have no merit of your own to plead why He should pardon you, but plead His written engagements and He will perform them. Are you afraid lest you should not be able to hold on to the end, lest, after having thought yourself a child of God, you should prove a castaway? If that is your state, take this word of grace to the throne and plead it: 'The mountains may depart, and the hills may be removed, but the covenant of My love shall not depart from thee.' If you have lost the sweet sense of the Saviour's presence, and are seeking Him with a sorrowful heart, remember the promises: 'Return unto Me, and I will return unto you; For a small moment have I forsaken thee, but with great mercies will I gather thee.' Banquet your faith upon God's own word, and whatever your fears or wants, repair to the Bank of Faith with your Father's note of hand, saying, 'Remember the word unto Thy servant, upon which Thou hast caused me to hope.'[2]

*My Story* continues
Emails to my intercessors:

August 2, 2015
Gabriel House requires a caregiver in attendance, separable only by a two-hour window from the 'caree.' This may pose a challenge for both of us. I am independent functionally, able to drive, etc. I suspect many residents are much sicker. I request your daily prayer during this time. I have marked my calendar with a small 'r' (for radiation

treatments) and a big 'J' (for Jesus): combined that puts the little 'r' under the big 'J' (Jr.) and that's where it should be. I pray the Lordship of Jesus over the entire treatment process from beginning to end (Jesus, the Alpha and the Omega), the destruction of the malignant cells and the protection of benign ones and vital organs. (Hebrews 4:12: 'For the word of God is sharper than any two-edged sword, and piercing as far as the division of soul and spirit, of both joints and marrow.') Also, no side effects. The rebuilding of my immune system. And a chance to share the gospel.

August 11, 2015

David and I share a room on the first floor of Gabriel House overlooking a lake with waterfowl and wrapped by tall pines that lift one's eyes and heart to heaven. A screened patio became our routine breakfast nook, a quiet, peaceful, healing setting.

Radiation treatments one through five are history. Twenty more to go. With God's grace, favor, and your prayers, I am doing well. My strength was bolstered by finding a local church, Eleven22. The teaching Sunday was 'God is greater than…*fear*.' Fear, not doubt, was defined as the opposite of faith. The teaching was from Numbers 14:9, two faithful spies that saw the giants, but recognized, '…they are bread for us.' I went forward for prayer after the service, and it was a powerful deliverance. I felt afterward, I could take on a lion.

August 20, 2015

Beloved intercessors,

Today marks the official half-way point of radiation treatment. I've already asked if I can say '*Stop*!' mid-treatment and go to Starbucks and celebrate. Of course, the answer was '*No…after*.' I saw the radiation oncology doctor yesterday who affirmed the present plan to stop at treatment #25, September 8th, and said that I was doing well. The kidney in jeopardy has been shielded and may return to a normal anatomical position, and possibly be spared, as well as the proposed colon resection which margin bordered the tumor. The surgeon will make that call on sight.

I am honored to have been asked to do a daily prayer walk through Gabriel House by the Christian director, after we discussed spiritual warfare, principalities, and powers. Please stand with me in praying Ephesians 6.

Gabriel House of Care is larger than I first described. There are twenty-nine private rooms that can accommodate one to three caregiver/guests. The transplant patients are separate, on the second floor. We all share four industrial kitchens on the first floor with refrigerator and pantry space assigned. A favorite event is 'The Chef is In,' nights where church, civic, and community groups prepare and cater an entire meal, usually bi-weekly. Tonight is pizza night!

David is doing well also. A friend from Gainesville visits regularly and he has bonded with another young male caregiver, and they have gone fishing on the St. John's River.

Current prayer needs are for the Lord's continuing favor, healing and protection, housing during the month off between the end of radiation and surgery (September 9 to October 8), direction to the right services and applications that can provide financial assistance with the Mayo 35% co-pay.

Love in Him, Trudy

# CHAPTER EIGHT

---

## The eighth "P" is for *His Power.*

Philippians 3:10:
"…and the power of His resurrection…"

---

In Chapter One, *His Purpose*, we studied Philippians 3:10, "…that I may know Him…" This verse continues "…and the power of His resurrection…"

The power of the Lord is with you, the believer, available everywhere you go. God gives us power to become His children first (John 1:12); power over all the power of the enemy (Luke 10:19); power to heal all kinds of sickness and disease (Matthew 10:1); and power to be His witnesses (Acts 1:8) "…in the power of signs and wonders, in the power of the Spirit (Romans 15:19); and, as in Philippians 3:10, "…the power of His resurrection." That latter Scripture will be our primary focus in this chapter. The resurrection power of Christ Jesus, our risen Savior and Lord (John 20:1-15) gives us the power over sickness and death in our bodies (Romans 8:11) and the boldness to believe to pray in faith for others. And we will conclude this chapter's study with Proverbs 18:21: "Death and life are in the power of the tongue…" (KJV), as it applies to our cancer battle.

## A. RESURRECTION POWER

Luke 24:49: "And behold, I am sending forth the promise of My Father upon you; but you are to stay in the city until you are clothed with *power* from on high" (Emphasis mine).

The disciples tarried in Jerusalem ten days after the ascension of Christ until the day of Pentecost when the Holy Spirit came upon them, Acts 2:1-4:

> When the day of Pentecost had come, they were all together in one place. 2 And suddenly there came from heaven a noise like a violent rushing wind, and it filled the whole house where they were sitting. 3 And there appeared to them tongues as of fire distributing themselves, and they rested on each one of them.
> 4 And they were all filled with the Holy Spirit and began to speak with other tongues, as the Spirit was giving them utterance.

From the Greek New Testament this power is *dunamis* (doo'-nam-is), dynamite: "force (literally or figuratively); specially, miraculous power (usually by implication, a miracle itself). KJV: ability, abundance, meaning, might (-ily, -y, -y deed), (worker of) miracle (-), power, strength, violence, mighty (wonderful) work."[1]

Let's look at the story of Jesus' resurrection, the cornerstone of our Christian faith, the demonstration of this *dunamis* power of the Holy Spirit in John 20:1-18.

## Resurrection!

Early in the morning on the first day of the week, while it was still dark, Mary Magdalene came to the tomb and saw that the stone was moved away from the entrance. 2 She ran at once to Simon Peter and the other disciple, the one Jesus loved, breathlessly panting, 'They took the Master from the tomb. We don't know where they've put him.'

3 Peter and the other disciple left immediately for the tomb. 4 They ran, neck and neck. The other disciple got to the tomb first, outrunning Peter.

5 Stooping to look in, he saw the pieces of linen cloth lying there, but he didn't go in. 6 Simon Peter arrived after him, entered the tomb, observed the linen cloths lying there, 7 and the kerchief used to cover his head not lying with the linen cloths but separate, neatly folded by itself. 8 Then the other disciple, the one who had gotten there first, went into the tomb, took one look at the evidence, and believed. 9 No one yet knew from the Scripture that he had to rise from the dead.[2] 10 The disciples then went back home. 11 But Mary stood outside the tomb weeping. As she wept, she knelt to look into the tomb 12 and saw two angels sitting there, dressed in white, one at the head, the other at the foot of where Jesus' body had been laid. 13 They said to her, 'Woman, why do you weep?'

'They took my Master,' she said, 'and I don't know where they put him.' 14 After she said this, she turned away and saw Jesus standing there. But she didn't recognize him.

15 Jesus spoke to her, 'Woman, why do you weep? Who are you looking for?' She, thinking that he was the gardener, said, 'Mister, if you took him, tell me where you put him so I can care for him.'

16 Jesus said, 'Mary.' Turning to face him, she said in Hebrew, 'Rabboni!' meaning 'Teacher!'

17 Jesus said, 'Don't cling to me, for I have not yet ascended to the Father. Go to my brothers and tell them, 'I ascend to my Father and your Father, my God and your God.' 18 Mary Magdalene went, telling the news to the disciples: 'I saw the Master!' And she told them everything he said to her (The Message).

And beloved, the good news is that the same Spirit that raised Jesus from the dead in *dunamis* power can indwell you, the believer. Romans 8:11 says:

"But if the Spirit of Him who raised Jesus from the dead dwells in _____, He who raised Christ Jesus from the dead will also give life to _____mortal bodies through His Spirit who dwells in _____." (you, your, you)

We have studied the names of God: Jesus (*Savior*) and Christ (*The Anointed One*). As Savior, He has the power to save (*sozo*). And in life, as The Anointed One, he has the power over sickness and in resurrection, the power over death (John 20:1-18). I believe, dear one, a diagnosis of cancer of you or your loved one is a death assignment from the enemy. Let me explain.

Can we know His power over and through cancer? Yes, even cancer. Have you asked yet why you need a cancer battle plan? If so, let me answer that first for you.

Man, a tripartite being, is body, soul, and spirit. Disease in our body can be a symptom possibly pointing to an underlying root, a weakened immune system. But what caused it to weaken? Underlying dis-ease in our soul (mind, will, and emotions) or in our spirit?

Stress, fear and/or anxiety, unforgiveness of self or others leading to a root of bitterness or self-hatred can cause sickness in the soul.

From the fall of Adam and Eve in the garden, sin, one's separation from God, causes sickness of the spirit. A New Testament example of the latter can be found in Matthew 9:2-7:

> And they brought to Him a paralytic lying on a bed. Seeing their faith, Jesus said to the paralytic, 'Take courage, son; your sins are forgiven.' 3 And some of the scribes said to themselves, 'This fellow blasphemes.' 4 And Jesus knowing their thoughts said, 'Why are you thinking evil in your hearts? 5 Which is easier, to say, 'Your sins are forgiven,' or to say, 'Get up, and walk?' 6 'But so that you may know that the Son of Man has authority on earth to forgive sins'—then He said to the paralytic, 'Get up, pick up your bed and go home.' 7 And he got up and went home. 8 But when the crowds saw this, they were awestruck, and glorified God, who had given such authority to men.

We need a cancer battle plan, beloved, because Scripture says we are in a war. And in a war, there can be casualties. Casualties can be our bodies, souls, or spirits. With a cancer diagnosis, I believe we battle a spirit of death and infirmity.

> For though we walk in the flesh, we do not *war* after the flesh: 4 For the weapons of our warfare are not carnal, but mighty through God to the pulling down of strongholds;
> 5 Casting down imaginations, and every high thing that exalteth itself against the knowledge of God, and bringing into captivity every thought to the obedience of Christ…(2 Corinthians 10:3-5, KJV, emphasis mine).

If we believe 2 Corinthians 10:3-5 that we are indeed in a war, who and where is our enemy? Since Eden, disguised as a serpent, our enemy has been the devil. Study Genesis 3:14-15:

> "God told the serpent: 'Because you've done this, you're cursed,
>     cursed beyond all cattle and wild animals,
> Cursed to slink on your belly and eat dirt all your life.
> 15 I'm declaring *war* between you and the Woman,
>     between your offspring and hers"
> (The Message, emphasis mine).

> "For we wrestle not against flesh and blood, but against principalities, against powers, against the rulers of the darkness of this world, against spiritual wickedness in high places" (Ephesians 6:12, KJV).

"Principalities and powers," answers "the who," but where is the enemy?

Ephesians 6:12 describes that we wrestle with an invisible realm, "not against flesh and blood, but against rulers of the darkness of this world, against spiritual wickedness in high places."

But we need not fear a defeated enemy. See Colossians 2:12-15:

> ...in which *you also were raised with Him through faith in the working of God, who raised Him from the dead.* 13 And you, being dead in your trespasses and the uncircumcision of your flesh, He has made alive together with Him, having forgiven you all trespasses, 14 having wiped out the handwriting of requirements that was against us, which was contrary to us. And He has taken it out of the way, having nailed it to the cross. 15 *Having disarmed principalities and powers, He made a public spectacle of them, triumphing over them in it* (NKJV, emphasis mine).

"Having disarmed principalities and powers, He made a public spectacle of them, triumphing over them..." Yes, Satan was defeated at the cross of Calvary by Jesus. Then why must we still war?

God had given the Promised Land to Israel, but they still had to dispossess the occupants of the land to take possession. Any territory where evil, sin, sickness, destruction have gained a foothold in your life, beloved, you can and must take back and maintain possession.

God has given us powerful weapons, offensive and defensive, to overcome the power of our enemy. And we will study them in depth in the next chapter, *His Protection*. But the most powerful is His Holy Spirit, resident in us, the very same Holy Spirit that raised Jesus from the dead.

As Jesus' resurrection from the dead is the cornerstone of Christian faith, do you, dear reader, believe God raised Jesus from the dead by the power of the Holy Spirit?

I pray for me and for you, revelation knowledge, or a deeper one, of John 20:1-18 and Romans 8:11:

> "But if the Spirit of Him who raised Jesus from the dead dwells in you, He who raised Christ Jesus from the dead will also give life to your mortal bodies through His Spirit who dwells in you."

Beloved, if the same power of the Holy Spirit dwells in you that raised Christ Jesus from the dead, you have all the power you will ever need to walk in fullness of life and health. Ask the Holy Spirit to give you this Power, Himself, if you have not already asked in Chapter Two, *His Preparation*. Ask for revelation knowledge of this power working inside you. What confidence then we would have to pray for the sick and to walk in Divine health ourselves.

## B. THE POWER OF THE TONGUE, THE AUTHORITY OF THE BELIEVER

> "Death and life are in the power of the tongue..." (Proverbs 18:21, KJV).

Have you ever spoken the opposite of God's truth, a lie, over your body? I have, beloved. I've felt parts of my body were ugly. An example, my feet. I've thought/said: "Some people have pretty feet. I don't." Or I've thought or spoken: "I hate my____." Fill in the blank if you have too. Then I applied truth, Scriptures I had found:

> "...How beautiful are the feet of them that preach the gospel of peace, and bring glad tidings of good things!" (Romans 10:15, KJV).

And another:

Psalm 139:14-16:
"I will give thanks to You, for I am fearfully and wonderfully made;
Wonderful are Your works,
And my soul knows it very well.
15 My frame was not hidden from You,
When I was made in secret,
And skillfully wrought in the depths of the earth;
16 Your eyes have seen my unformed substance…"

I repented of my envy of others that I had compared myself to. I repeated those Scriptures over and over until I came to believe them in my heart, not just my head. And I confessed them with my mouth.

In your cancer battle what have you spoken over yourself? The doctor's prognosis? *Jehovah-rophe* is *The Lord, Physician*. Get His opinion. I have been very careful, not just in this book, but in every medical context, not to "name and claim" the diagnosis. It started with the neurosurgeon who called the meningioma, "the thing in your head." I liked that but still told very few people the doctor's diagnosis, not wanting pity. And with cancer, I defined the problem as "the doctor's report." I recall lyrics to a Christian song: "*Whose report will you believe? I believe the report of the Lord.*" We always have a choice. As a medical professional, I don't deny the doctor's words, but submit them to a higher Power.

Remember from Chapter Five, *His Peace*, the war on cancer begins with our very thoughts: "…taking every thought captive to the obedience of Christ…" (2 Corinthians 10:5). This is important because "What you say flows from what is in your heart" (Luke 6:45, New Living Translation).

Jesus said, "I am the resurrection and the life…" (John 11:25). Remember in Chapter One, *His Purpose*, that to be saved you confessed with your mouth Jesus as Lord and believed in your heart that God raised Jesus from the dead (Romans 10:9). Speak life over your body, soul, and spirit. Surround yourself with people who do likewise. Get healing Scriptures on CD and play them on repeat, night and day; saturate the very walls of your house and heart.

Remember that you exercise your power in Him by speaking His Word, our authority as believers. Before Jesus gave His disciples *dunamis* power (Acts 2), He gave them *exousia*, authority (Matthew 10:1, Luke 10:19-20).

From the Greek-Hebrew, *exousia* (ex-oo-see'-ah); is defined: "(in the sense of ability); privilege, i.e. (subjectively) force, capacity, competency, freedom, or (objectively) mastery (concretely, magistrate, super-human, potentate, token of control), delegated influence. KJV: authority, jurisdiction, liberty, power, right, strength."[3]

Matthew 10:1:
"Jesus summoned His twelve disciples and gave them _____ over unclean spirits, to cast them out, and to heal every kind of disease and every kind of sickness." (authority)

Luke 10:19–20:
"Behold, I give you the _____ to trample on serpents and scorpions, and over all the power of the enemy, and nothing shall by any means hurt you.

20 Nevertheless do not rejoice in this, that the spirits are subject to you, but rather rejoice because your names are written in heaven" (NKJV). (authority)

James 5:17-18 quotes a story example of *exousia*:

"Elijah was a man with a nature like ours, and he prayed earnestly that it would not rain; and it did not rain on the land for three years and six months. 18 And he prayed again, and the heaven gave rain, and the earth produced its fruit" (NKJV).

Read it in its entirety in I Kings 17-18.

Life Application

Scripture Memory Verse
Romans 8:11:

_____

_____

_____

_____

"But if the Spirit of Him who raised Jesus from the dead dwells in you, He who raised Christ Jesus from the dead will also give life to your mortal bodies through His Spirit who dwells in you."

How have you experienced God's power?

_____

_____

_____

How do you need to experience God's power now?

_____

_____

_____

Practice *exousia* in those areas where the Lord has given you delegated authority: your body, soul, spirit, and your household. And study the gospels, the accounts of Jesus' and His disciples' "going." Look for patterns. He promises signs and wonders shall follow believers (Acts 2:43) and He says that we, His disciples, shall do greater works than He (John 14:12). As your faith grows, look for ways you, too, can exercise the *dunamis* power of the Holy Spirit.

*My Story*
Emails to my intercessors:

September 8, 2015
Dear intercessors:

Rejoice with me.

I finished radiation treatment #25 today. Praise the Lord! All is well. Thank you for your thoughts and prayers. I couldn't have done it without you!

Love in Him, Trudy

September 26, 2015
Dear intercessors,

Prayer answers and needs

How are you? It's so good to hear from you when you are able to respond. I stayed in Jacksonville for the month between treatments, radiation and upcoming surgery, because of the possibility of 'soaking prayer.' There is a Healing Prayer Room located here and I was not disappointed. I came by walk-in rather than appointment. Two prayer ministers spent approximately twenty minutes with me. One herself had been in intercession three hours that morning, asking God for a healing miracle that day. They felt a powerful anointing when they prayed for me and did lay hands on the tumor site. I hope to be that miracle in whatever way gives God most glory.

Monday, September 28, starts my pre-op evaluation at 8 a.m.: labs, EKG, kidney function test, consents, and paperwork. Tuesday, September 29, continues the process with 5:45 a.m. MRI of abdomen and pelvis followed by a CT of same, a chest X-ray, and appointments with both the oncologist and surgeon. Surgery is scheduled for October 8.

God's perfect will is my desire. Prayer needs include housing on discharge from Mayo Hospital post-surgery. That might be for about two weeks (till follow-up appointment and discharge completely from Mayo services). With a caregiver I could return to Gabriel House, but David is presently working part-time in Gainesville, a 1.5-hour commute.

Blessings, Trudy

October 7, 2015
Dear intercessors,

Eve of surgery. Thank you for your continuing prayers.

I have pre-typed your addresses in my email draft for contact follow-up. I will ask my sons Jonathan and David to access this post-surgery until I am able. Schedule reminder: admission to Mayo 5:15 a.m. October 8, Thursday; surgery at 7:15 a.m.

A urologist will do the ureter stents and my surgeon, Dr. Bagaria, the rest.

I have found an affordable apartment in Jacksonville again with a month-to-month lease, that even allows me David's cat Victor. One intercessor calls him 'Victory.' I like that. He'll be good company for the next month that I've been asked to stay in Jacksonville by the surgeon for follow-up.

Thank you for your faithfulness and encouragement. You have blessed me more than you will ever know until eternity.

Love, Trudy


October 8, 2015
Day of surgery, David posted:


Dear intercessors,

This is a pre-written communication, to keep in touch and let you know God answers prayer. Before surgery, I pictured myself like Queen Esther in the book of Esther, coming before *THE KING* and my petition, as hers, being my very life. And like Esther, *THE KING* extended His golden scepter and granted my request (John10:10). All is well. More to follow.

In Him, Trudy


October 14, 2015
Dear, dear intercessors,

Update Post-surgery

Your prayers were invaluable. Thank you. The surgery October 8 removed a ten-pound tumor, a liposarcoma, my right kidney, and part of my colon. It lasted eight hours. The surgeon felt he removed 100% of the cancer, left clean borders. Bleeding was minimal, and no post-op complications. Recovery has been a battle again with nausea as during radiation, also pain. I am expected to be discharged today to a skilled nursing facility for possibly twenty days. The Lord had woken up an intercessor one night with the thought I'd need a skilled nursing facility for rehabilitation rather than an apartment where I would have been living independently at this time.

Love and blessings, Trudy

# CHAPTER NINE

---

## The ninth "P" is for *His Protection.*

Psalm 91:11:
"For He will give His angels charge concerning you, to guard you in all
your ways…"

---

Preparing to go on outreach, and hearing from Loren Cunningham that YWAM medical teams go into some of the most dangerous places in the world, I came across this:

NEWS Report from Loren Cunningham, Youth with a Mission founder.

Taliban-trained militants were sent from Iran to this region and two months ago, they marched to within 300 yards of one of our YWAM campuses, wielding destruction all along the way. They were blood-thirsty, having already burned 27 Christian churches in the area, some with people inside (we have seen heart wrenching photos taken by YWAMers of charred bodies of martyrs in burned out churches, plus mass graves). Approximately 1,000 Christians were killed within a few hours.

God protected our very brave and totally committed YWAMers…The YWAM Discipleship Training School outreach that concluded September 30th, after much prayer, knew God was leading them on outreach to the camps of the militants who were killing, kidnapping, bombing, using grenade-launchers, etc. Into the camps went the YWAMers, prayed up, ready to die or see God's power. They saw God's power! One of the most ruthless murderers, armed with a large knife, approached the YWAMers with his knife poised over his head. The other militants had seen that when he went into this demonic rage, he didn't stop until he had killed someone, so they said to the YWAMers 'run!' The school leader, Alex, said 'no,' and started walking toward the man. Alex spoke firmly but calmly, 'You need Jesus.' Over and over, he said it, as he drew closer to the drawn knife's point. The man replied 'No! Run or you die!' When Alex was just a few feet away, the man fell to his knees, threw down his weapon and began weeping. He was saved and delivered, as were many others.

Loren
October 7, 2009, Nigeria.[1]

Is this testimony of God's power and protection unusual and an exception? Let's look at the life of Jesus in the New Testament. How did God, the Father, protect His only son, Jesus, from premature death before His purpose and plan of salvation could be accomplished on the cross?

Matthew 2:1-15:

Now after Jesus was born in Bethlehem of Judea in the days of Herod the king, magi from the east arrived in Jerusalem, saying, 2 'Where is He who has been born King of the Jews? For we saw His star in the east and have come to worship Him.' 3 When Herod the king heard this, he was troubled, and all Jerusalem with him. 4 Gathering together all the chief priests and scribes of the people, he inquired of them where the Messiah was to be born. 5 They said to him, 'In Bethlehem of Judea; for this is what has been written by the prophet:

6 'AND YOU, BETHLEHEM, LAND OF JUDAH, ARE BY NO MEANS LEAST AMONG THE LEADERS OF JUDAH; FOR OUT OF YOU SHALL COME FORTH A RULER WHO WILL SHEPHERD MY PEOPLE ISRAEL.'

7 Then Herod secretly called the magi and determined from them the exact time the star appeared. 8 And he sent them to Bethlehem and said, 'Go and search carefully for the Child; and when you have found Him, report to me, so that I too may come and worship Him.' 9 After hearing the king, they went their way; and the star, which they had seen in the east, went on before them until it came and stood over the place where the Child was. 10 When they saw the star, they rejoiced exceedingly with great joy. 11 After coming into the house they saw the Child with Mary His mother; and they fell to the ground and worshiped Him. Then, opening their treasures, they presented to Him gifts of gold, frankincense, and myrrh. 12 And having been warned by God in a dream not to return to Herod, the magi left for their own country by another way.

13 Now when they had gone, behold, an angel of the Lord appeared to Joseph in a dream and said, 'Get up! Take the Child and His mother and flee to Egypt, and remain there until I tell you; for Herod is going to search for the Child to destroy Him.'

14 So Joseph got up and took the Child and His mother while it was still night, and left for Egypt. 15 He remained there until the death of Herod. This was to fulfill what had been spoken by the Lord through the prophet: 'OUT OF EGYPT I CALLED MY SON.'

In Matthew 2:13 we read that Joseph was warned by God in a dream to flee to Egypt. What was his response? See Matthew 2:14:

_____

_____

_____

_____

Immediate obedience! In the middle of the night. Obedience keeps us in the center of God's will, the place of His protection and power.

Let's look at another example, an Old Testament one, the story of another Deliverer, Moses. How did God spare Moses' life? Exodus 1:22-2:10:

> Then Pharaoh commanded all his people, saying, 'Every son who is born you are to cast into the Nile, and every daughter you are to keep alive.'
>
> Now a man from the house of Levi went and married a daughter of Levi. 2 The woman conceived and bore a son; and when she saw that he was beautiful, she hid him for three months. 3 But when she could hide him no longer, she got him a wicker basket and covered it over with tar and pitch. Then she put the child into it and set it among the reeds by the bank of the Nile. 4 His sister stood at a distance to find out what would happen to him.
>
> 5 The daughter of Pharaoh came down to bathe at the Nile, with her maidens walking alongside the Nile; and she saw the basket among the reeds and sent her maid, and she brought it to her. 6 When she opened it, she saw the child, and behold, the boy was crying. And she had pity on him and said, 'This is one of the Hebrews' children.' 7 Then his sister said to Pharaoh's daughter, 'Shall I go and call a nurse for you from the Hebrew women that she may nurse the child for you?' 8 Pharaoh's daughter said to her, 'Go ahead.' So the girl went and called the child's mother. 9 Then Pharaoh's daughter said to her, 'Take this child away and nurse him for me and I will give you your wages.' So the woman took the child and nursed him. 10 The child grew, and she brought him to Pharaoh's daughter and he became her son. And she named him Moses, and said, 'Because I drew him out of the water.'

Moses' mother did not have the New Testament example of the story of Joseph being warned in a dream that spared the life of the Christ-child. Yet, she knew the God of her fathers, Abraham, Isaac, and Jacob, and His covenant promises. How do you think she was led by God to attempt to spare Moses' life in this manner? Had she heard God's voice, seen a vision, had a dream? Or, as a mother, just loved this son as dearly as her own life? We can only imagine how a Godly Hebrew woman might have been led by God.

So, then what is our part? I believe it is found in studying and applying Ephesians 6:10-11:

> "Finally, my brethren, be strong in the Lord, and in the power of his might. 11 Put on the whole armour of God, that ye may be able to stand against the wiles of the devil" (KJV).

## A. THE ARMOR OF GOD

Ephesians 6:13-18 goes on to describe this in detail:

> Therefore, put on every piece of God's armor so you will be able to resist the enemy in the time of evil. Then after the battle you will still be standing firm. 14 Stand your ground, *putting on the belt of truth* and *the body armor of God's righteousness.* 15 *For shoes, put on the peace that comes from the Good News* so that you will be fully prepared. 16 In addition to all of these, *hold up the shield of faith to stop the fiery arrows of the devil.* 17 *Put on salvation as your helmet*, and *take the sword of the Spirit, which is the word of God.* 18 *Pray in the Spirit at all times and on every occasion.* Stay alert and be persistent in your prayers for all believers everywhere (New Living Translation, emphasis mine).

Let's examine each component of our armor separately.

### (1) *Putting on the belt of truth*

If you have studied military history, you may know that a loose garment was definitely not an asset in battle. A belt, the first part of the armor put on, was to secure tightly one's garment. What is the belt of truth in our spiritual armory? But a better question might be Pilates, "What is truth?" (John 18:38). *Truth*, as defined by Scripture, is a Person. Jesus spoke of Himself: "I am the way, the truth, and the life" (John 14:6). If we examine ourselves, searching ourselves with the spotlight of the Holy Spirit, are there any lies, the opposite of truth, we have believed that have weakened our armor and that we first need to repent of? Then put on the belt of truth tightly.

### (2) *The body armor of God's righteousness*

The Word, Jesus Himself, is my righteousness. This breastplate covers my chest, my heart. If I have invited Jesus into my heart, that piece is in place. And if I sin, repentance can restore me to His righteousness. But be sure you stand, "…having on the body armor of God's righteousness…" before you go into battle.

### (3) *Your feet shod with the peace that comes from the Good News*

Before I go into spiritual warfare, as in Communion, I first should examine myself. Am I at enmity with anyone? If the answer is "*Yes*," I should leave my gift at the altar and first be reconciled to my brother (Matthew 5:23-24). Then when God's peace umpires my heart, proceed and recover all (1 Samuel 30:8). David, a king, called for God's ephod to discern God's will before going into war (1 Samuel 30:7). Then shouldn't we, too? Yes, healing is "the children's bread" (Matthew 15:26).

### (4) *Above all* (NKJV) *hold up the shield of faith to stop the fiery arrows of the devil.*

Note, the preface, "Above all…" implies the highest priority of all. Why? Because if that's in place the fiery arrows will be deflected.

But what is a shield of faith? First, let us ask ourselves another question, "What is faith?" God answers from His Word, "…faith is the substance …evidence of things not seen" (Hebrews 11:1, KJV). Substance is matter, raw material and evidence is proof. That is a real commodity, beloved. So is our shield of faith. A shield of faith is visible in the spirit realm even to the enemy whose weapon is to attempt to instill fear based on lies, his being in the words of Jesus, "the father of lies" (John 8:44). You may have heard the acronym F. E. A. R. defined as *False Evidence Appearing Real*.

And His Word further says in Hebrews 11:6-12:

> And without faith it is impossible to please Him, for he who comes to God must believe that He is and that He is a rewarder of those who seek Him. 7 By faith Noah, being warned by God about things not yet seen, in reverence prepared an ark for the salvation of his household, by which he condemned the world, and became an heir of the righteousness which is according to faith.
>
> 8 By faith Abraham, when he was called, obeyed by going out to a place which he was to receive for an inheritance; and he went out, not knowing where he was going. 9 By faith he lived as an alien in the land of promise, as in a foreign land, dwelling in

tents with Isaac and Jacob, fellow heirs of the same promise; 10 for he was looking for the city which has foundations, whose architect and builder is God. 11 By faith even Sarah herself received ability to conceive, even beyond the proper time of life, since she considered Him faithful who had promised. 12 Therefore there was born even of one man, and him as good as dead at that, as many descendants AS THE STARS OF HEAVEN IN NUMBER, AND INNUMERABLE AS THE SAND WHICH IS BY THE SEASHORE.

Then how do we actually take up the shield of faith? Reading Ephesians 6 makes us aware of it. Praying Ephesians 6 is even better, visualizing each piece of our armor as we dress for the day. But Bible teacher Beth Moore has a practical way she applies the shield of faith. It consists of five "I believes…"[2] As she raises her right hand, she says, thumb up: "I believe God is who He says He is." As she raises the index finger, she adds "I believe God can do what He says He can do." Adds the middle finger, proclaiming, "I believe I am who God says I am." With the next finger raised, she says, "I believe I can do all things through Christ." And lastly, with the little finger, says, "God's word is alive and active in me." She follows this with sign language, pointing at her heart, "I," then her head, "believe," then up to heaven, "God." I believe God. That is powerful, and life-changing when it's practiced till it becomes a habit. I know.

So above all, take up the shield of faith. And with Beth Moore's model, I can examine myself against the five "I believes," to see which front the enemy is mounting an assault: against God's power, my position in Christ, or against His Word itself.

### (5) Put on salvation as your helmet

In Chapter Two, *His Preparation*, we studied the meanings of saved, *sozo*, as salvation (spirit), deliverance (soul), and healing of sickness and disease (body).

### (6) and take the sword of the Spirit, which is the Word of God.

As an undergraduate in the nursing program at the University of Pittsburgh, I chose fencing as my physical education elective. I would learn much later that the biblical meaning of my name, Gertrude, was "spear-maiden." And I would see that "warrior" develop as part of my identity. But even in practice with an epee', a thrust to the chest with the tip would smart long after. I recall, too, being introduced to the saber, even more impressive.

But in the spirit, our sword is the Word of God, Jesus, and His inspired Word, the Bible, as per Ephesians 6:17.

Unlike fencing, we can hold *the* sword in one hand and the spiritual shield of faith in the other simultaneously, deflecting all the blows of the enemy.

### (7) Pray in the Spirit at all times and on every occasion.

Prayer is one of the most powerful weapons we possess in our battle with Satan and we will examine this in Chapter Thirteen, *His Prayer*. I believe the name, Jesus, (*Savior*), spoken both in prayer and duress, has life-sustaining power, victory over all the forces of darkness. Satan has been called the prince of this world. "Greater is He that is in you, than he that is in the world" (1 John 4:4).

When I think of a protection prayer, I immediately go to Psalm 91. When my daughter was very young and afraid of the dark and sleeping alone in a big, dark room, I recited this psalm every night, inserting her name. She believed her name was printed in this psalm, as that was how she came to learn it. And her name, Maranatha, is in the Bible literally (1 Corinthians 16:23). When my son, David, a weekend Navy reservist, was re-activated and deployed to Afghanistan, we memorized it together. He sent me camouflage squares with it imprinted on that I made into worship/warfare banners.

Write it here from your favorite Bible translation. Please remember to insert your name wherever there is a pronoun reference to you, the believer. And this is My Prayer for You and your Scripture Memory Verse begun in Chapter Six, *His Presence*.

Psalm 91

_____

_____

_____

_____

_____

_____

_____

_____

_____

_____

_____

_____

_____

_____

_____

_____

_____

_____

_____

Remember the story of David, the young champion anointed by Samuel, who rose to the challenge of the giant Goliath? King Saul equipped him with armor. Let's look at the story in 1 Samuel 17:38-39:

"Then Saul clothed David with his garments and put a bronze helmet on his head, and he clothed him with armor. 39 David girded his sword over his armor and tried to walk, for he had not tested them. So David said to Saul, 'I cannot go with these, for I have not tested them.' And David took them off."

For a victorious battle, test your armor beforehand. Each battle plan of God's is unique. Remember Jericho, when after seven days of marching silently around the city, at the sound of a trumpet and shout, the walls, on the seventh day after seven marches that day, came down? Or in Moses' battle with the Amalekites, as long as his hands were raised, Israel was victorious. But God used a rock and Aaron and Hur to steady Moses' hands till sunset. We must use the Armor of God and follow His unique battle plan for our war on cancer.

## B. HOLY COMMUNION

Let's look at one more aspect of God's protection, His provision for you at the Last Supper of His very own body and blood.

Matthew 26:26-29:
The Lord's Supper Instituted

While they were eating, Jesus took some bread, and after a blessing, He broke it and gave it to the disciples, and said, 'Take, eat; this is My body.' 27 And when He had taken a cup and given thanks, He gave it to them, saying, 'Drink from it, all of you; 28 for this is My blood of the covenant, which is poured out for many for forgiveness of sins. 29 But I say to you, I will not drink of this fruit of the vine from now on until that day when I drink it new with you in My Father's kingdom.'

In this story Jesus takes bread, blesses it, and breaks it and gives to His disciples saying, "Take, eat..."
In another story in the gospels, we read that Jesus calls healing "...the children's bread." Look at Matthew 15:26-28:

"And He answered and said, 'It is not good to take the children's bread and throw it to the dogs.' 27 But she said, 'Yes, Lord; but even the dogs feed on the crumbs which fall from their masters' table.' 28 Then Jesus said to her, 'O woman, your faith is great; it shall be done for you as you wish.' And her daughter was healed at once."

Jesus says in John 6:48-51:

> "I am the bread of life. 49 Your fathers ate the manna in the wilderness, and they died. 50 This is the bread which comes down out of heaven, so that one may eat of it and not die. 51 I am the living bread that came down out of heaven; if anyone eats of this bread, he will live forever; and the bread also which I will give for the life of the world is My flesh."

And remember the Old Testament story of the Passover meal the night before the Israelites' exodus from Egypt after four-hundred-thirty years of slavery. The blood of a lamb, a prototype of Christ, called The Lamb of God, covered the doorposts and lintels of the houses, and after eating the lamb, no one any longer was sick or infirm (Psalms 105:37). That was prerequisite to their forty-year walk through the desert to the Promised Land. Our healing can also come this side of our promised land, heaven. I believe there is power in the Body and Blood of Jesus taken in remembrance of Him to heal every sickness and disease.

In *The Meal That Heals*, Perry Stone writes:

> During the first Passover, the flesh of a lamb was eaten at the table of the Hebrew family, and the lamb's flesh brought supernatural healing for the journey through the wilderness. The blood on the door stopped the destroying angel from taking the life of the Hebrew firstborn. Thus the body and blood of the Passover lamb brought complete healing and redemption.
>
> The body of Christ, God's final lamb, brought healing through the wounds and stripes on His body and salvation through His blood on the cross. Communion is a sign of belief in Christ's finished work and a testimony of faith in the complete work of salvation.[3]

Jesus also said, "…as oft as you do this, do this in remembrance of Me" (1 Corinthians 11:25).

1 Corinthians 11:23-26 reads:
…the Lord Jesus in the night in which He was betrayed took bread; 24 and when He had given thanks, He broke it and said, 'This is My body, which is for you; do this in remembrance of Me.' 25 In the same way He took the cup also after supper, saying, 'This cup is the new covenant in My blood; do this, as often as you drink it, in remembrance of Me.' 26 For as often as you eat this bread and drink the cup, you proclaim the Lord's death until He comes.

We, like the early church who broke bread daily from house to house, are also to do this frequently "…in remembrance of Me." By His stripes I am healed and by His blood I am cleansed and delivered from sin and death.

Life Application

Remember His name invokes His very Presence and promise(s). Remember Moses' battle with the Amalekites, *Jehovah-nissi, The Lord My Banner*, went before the Israelites. How have you known God's protection in your life?

_____

_____

_____

_____

Does your own Scriptural lifeline come to mind, a verse you go to over and over? Which one(s)? If so, take that into your next battle.

_____

_____

_____

_____

Did it require your obedience? If so, what was the result?

_____

_____

_____

_____

In Hebrew, *Jehovah-nissi* is *The Lord Is My Banner*. Webster defines "banner" as "a flag, originally the standard of a king" and "a piece of cloth bearing a design, motto, slogan…sometimes attached to a staff and used as a battle standard." Exodus 17:10-16 is a Scriptural example. Israel was battling the Amalekites. Moses stood on top of a hill overlooking the battle with the staff of God raised in his hand. As long as his hands were lifted, Israel was winning. When they lowered in fatigue, the Amalekites were winning. So, Aaron and Hur set Moses on a rock and held his hands steady until sunset. Israel prevailed. Are you set upon The Rock? Sunset may seem a long way off. Have you needed an Aaron and Hur in your battle(s)? Has God provided them? Where and when?

_____

_____

_____

_____

In summary, the Lord has shown me four principles of His protection that go with the believer. We, God's new covenant people, must literally go into battle too, knowing that the Lord's protection is: (1) the equipment of His army. From the book of Ephesians, we see He has given us a sword—His word (Ephesians 6:17); a shield—faith (6:16); a helmet—salvation (6:17); a breastplate—righteousness (6:14); a belt—truth (6:14); and fitted our feet with the gospel of peace (6:15). (2) The direction of our battles is determined by the position of the praisers holding up the staff of God (Exodus 17, Moses' battle with the Amalekites, Aaron and Hur holding up his hands). (3) The battle is the Lord's (1 Samuel 17:47, David's battle with a giant). (4) And we have a "secret weapon," praying in the Spirit (Ephesians 6:18). Meditate on these. Test your armor before the battle(s). Declare into your future what God has done for you in the past. Your remembrance builds your faith that He is able and willing to do it again.

2 Corinthians 10:3-4:
"For though we walk in the flesh, we do not war according to the flesh, 4 for the weapons of our warfare are not of the flesh, but divinely powerful for the destruction of fortresses."

God's protection is ultimately His Presence with His people. No enemy can overcome the power of God. His armies are hosts of angels who encamp around those who fear Him (Psalm 34:7). I am His beloved and His banner over me is love (Song of Songs 2:4). Go…in the Lord's protection.

Test Yourself
*Jehovah-nissi* means

_____

_____

*My Story*
Emails to my intercessors:

October 17, 2015
Dear intercessors,

Skilled Nursing Facility (SNF) Update
I am doing well. The battle is the Lord's. We have won the war! Praise God. I write to you on a beautiful, turning-fall day in Florida. I am at a SNF, a five-star, Medicare-approved one. In rehab, all rooms are private. I have a window. The assisted living adjoining is hosting a Fall Festival today, promising bratwurst and sauerkraut and apple cider. It will be a nice diet change!

I was admitted here on October 14 and expected to be here 10-14 days. I have Physical Therapy (PT) and Occupational Therapy (OT) daily and am making slow but steady progress in activities of daily living. There is an outdoor courtyard for PT, simulating a neighborhood terrain with its accompanying challenges. Also, a practice kitchen and laundry to reassess skills (OT).

My pain is controlled by round-the-clock medication, but nausea has resurfaced. So, I am trying to find a balance to still that storm without greater breakthrough pain on refusing pain medication. My appetite is finicky but improving. And pain medication also causes constipation. Another prayer need is housing after discharge here. I see the Mayo doctors on November 10, and have been asked to stay in Jacksonville until then. Travel to my son Jonathan in Kentucky is next. I asked to visit him for six months and he agreed. A long car ride (12 hours) requires hourly stops, and I'm thinking two days. Flying is an option, but luggage and airport terminal connections could even be more challenging.

Thank you for your encouragement, love, and prayers.

Numbers 6:24-26 Blessings, Trudy

October 27, 2015 Aaron and Hur…still needed on my behalf.

Exodus 17:8-13: Then Amalek came and fought against Israel at Rephidim. 9 So Moses said to Joshua, 'Choose men for us and go out, fight against Amalek. Tomorrow I will station myself on the top of the hill with the staff of God in my hand.' 10 Joshua did as Moses told him, and fought against Amalek; and Moses went up to the top of the hill. 11 So it came about when Moses held his hand up, that Israel prevailed, and when he let his hand down, Amalek prevailed. 12 But Moses's hands were heavy. Then they took a stone and put it under him, and he sat on it; and Aaron and Hur supported his hands, one on one side and one on the other. Thus his hands were steady until the sun set. 13 So Joshua overwhelmed Amalek and his people with the edge of the sword.

The battles have been steady. Sunday mid-sternal chest pain, nausea and shortness of breath caused concern that I might need re-hospitalization. This was averted as the symptoms turned out to be gastric and relieved by intervention here. A urinary tract infection was diagnosed, and I am on Cipro. Going off the pain medication completely has restored bowel function. Presently, my blood pressure drops markedly between lying, sitting, and standing, which has interrupted PT, except bed exercises.

Thank you for your continuing prayers.

Love, Trudy

# CHAPTER TEN

---

## The tenth "P" is for *His Prosperity*.

3 John 2 (KJV):
"Beloved, I wish above all things that thou mayest prosper and be in health,
even as thy soul prospereth."

---

Let's look together at another familiar Bible story.

> After coming into the house they saw the Child with Mary His mother; and they fell to the ground and worshiped Him. Then, opening their treasures, they presented to Him gifts of gold, frankincense, and myrrh. 12 And having been warned by God in a dream not to return to Herod, the magi left for their own country by another way.
>
> 13 Now when they had gone, behold, an angel of the Lord appeared to Joseph in a dream and said, 'Get up! Take the Child and His mother and flee to Egypt, and remain there until I tell you; for Herod is going to search for the Child to destroy Him.'
>
> 14 So Joseph got up and took the Child and His mother while it was still night, and left for Egypt. 15 He remained there until the death of Herod. This was to fulfill what had been spoken by the Lord through the prophet: 'OUT OF EGYPT I CALLED MY SON' (Matthew 2:11-15).

God's call to "go" is always accompanied by the circumstances that will enable you to be obedient. And gifts often accompany it. The gift of gold provided the money that Joseph, a carpenter, needed to travel immediately. There was no time to go back home for money or clothing or the tools he would need to start a business in Egypt. God's prosperity was timely and essential to spare the Child's life and fulfill His plan of salvation.

Yes, dear one, even "going" through the circumstances surrounding cancer yourself or a loved one, look for God's gifts. I remember the urgency with which the medical DTS staff seemingly propelled me to return to the mainland. And before I did, the wisdom shared with me to have medical follow-up in place. And the offer of housing from a fellow YWAMer near Mayo main campus. And my son's invitation to Florida where he would see me through this treatment process. So, housing was in place temporarily. And transportation. David came to drive me back to Florida, leaving my car with a friend again. My primary physician expedited the referral to Mayo Clinic, Jacksonville, Florida. And the oncologist there called the very next day. Treatment-wise, I was on a fast tract, my wait short, the first working day after the July Fourth holiday. The radiologist was the former head of Radiology, Rochester. All of this, I believe, God's fingerprints, His gifts to prosper me on my way to and through my treatment process.

This may not be your definition of prosperity. But cancer can be a life-or-death situation and treatment may have urgency. So, from that perspective, how is God prospering you during your or a loved one's cancer treatment process?

_____

_____

_____

_____

And looking at the process, can you see "gifts" along the way? And if so, what are they?

_____

_____

_____

_____

The unique gifts that God gives each of us are a way of prospering us, too, to go. In the desert, when God rained manna on the children of Israel, their first question was "…What is it?" (Exodus 16:15). Do we also fail to recognize the daily bread our Father provides? What is our yardstick to measure prosperity—the lifestyle of the rich and famous, our neighbor's blessings, or our own in relation to our needs, God's purpose and plan for our lives to be *Jehovah-jireh*, proportional in increase to our stewardship (Matthew 25:14-30), and the principle of sowing and reaping (2 Corinthians 9:6)?

There is a difference between the Giver, Himself, and the gift, prosperity. It is important to learn the difference. In our cancer battle, we would likely define prosperity as healing. Cancer seems to be no respecter of persons, rich or poor, famous, or unknown. I heard Natalie Grant, a vocalist, being interviewed on KLOVE, a Christian radio station, about a recent release, "More Than Anything." She had not written the words, but recorded them, and then was asked to re-release the song at a later time. Then, unknown to anyone else, she had just been diagnosed with thyroid cancer. A vocalist with thyroid cancer! I want to share her words and then her link to the song:

> …My prayer for 2018: JESUS more than anything—but as we all know, that sure is easier to say than it is to actually live.
> Oh Jesus, help us seek your face before we seek your hand. Help us to love you because of WHO YOU ARE, not because of what you can do for us. Two years ago, I recorded a song about this very thing, called "More Than Anything." The lyrics were inspired by the story of a woman battling a horrific cancer, yet her heart's cry was 'I know you can heal me Lord, but even if you choose not to in this life, help me want the Healer,

more than the healing.' I'll never forget being in the studio, and as I recorded this song, I was thinking of many people who were facing the unthinkable. I prayed it become a lifeline—JESUS more than anything.

Fast forward a couple of years to this past August. My record Company came to me and said they wanted to make this song my new release to radio, 'Awesome,' I thought. And I began to pray again that it would push people towards the only answer: JESUS.

But then September came.

And I was diagnosed with cancer.

I was set to sing this song for a huge radio conference the same week of my diagnosis, and as I was rehearsing, I got to the lyrics chorus: help me want the Healer, more than the healing...I couldn't get the words out. 'No!', I screamed in my mind. 'No! No! No!' This song was for someone else's story. This song was to help someone else. But God knew back in 2015 when I recorded it, that He was going to help me learn to live it two years later.

And so I walked out on that stage and sang this song. And I felt like such a fraud, because honestly, I just wanted the healing. But I so tangibly and sincerely felt Him say: 'get your mind off your circumstances and focus your eyes on ME. Stop thinking of all that you need me to do for you, and start thinking about WHO I AM. Write it down, say it out loud. Do it continually and it will take root.'

And so I did.

You are my Savior.

You are my Father.

You are my Healer.

You are my Protector.

You are my Provider.

You are faithful.

You are kind.

You are good.

You are sovereign.

Your love knows no end...

His truth brings silence to the noise.

Our outcomes do not determine His goodness. As I focused on HIM and Him alone, I began to experience His peace that completely passes understanding. I'm talking about a calm in the depth of my soul that doesn't even make sense. I actually felt His nearness in a way I had never experienced before. I encountered His presence in a way I never knew possible. This is WHO HE IS—personal, always reaching, always pursuing. In order to go higher, we must go deeper. Sometimes it takes walking through the valley of the shadow of death to get us there...

No matter what we are in the middle of, God is already THERE...[1]

Here's a link to my song on iTunes. I hope it grabs ahold of your heart and mind. http://smarturl.it/iTunesMoreThan[2]

In 1 Samuel 18:14, we see David's walk with the Lord described, "And David was prospering in all his ways for the Lord was with him." Therefore, the first way the Lord prospers you when you "go" is with His Presence. Psalm 35:27 says "...The Lord be magnified, who delights in the prosperity of His servant." I believe the key word is *servant*. When we are about our Father's business, then we, like David, are after God's heart.

Secondly, the Lord prospers you with His blessing when you go. He always blesses obedience to His word. In fact, I believe it is the only place the Lord can bless us. Proverbs 10:22 says, "It is the blessing of the Lord that makes rich and He adds no sorrow to it." I believe prosperity is a kingdom principle. But a law of the kingdom is only the law of the land where He is King.

Your Scripture Memory Verses

"But seek first His kingdom and His righteousness, and all these
things will be added to you" (Matthew 6:33).

"Delight yourself in the Lord; And He will give you the desires of your heart" (Psalm 37:4).

*My Story*

March 12, 2016
Dear intercessors,

To God be the glory...

...great things He has done.

Those of you who walked alongside of me my recent journey, may remember how I was led to Mayo Clinic, Jacksonville, Florida from Youth With a Mission, Kona, Hawaii...But on arrival at Mayo, I found they did not accept Medicare consignment, and could charge more. As my mail couldn't be forwarded from University of the Nations, Kona, a business, Mayo Clinic could not find a way for Medicare's direct payments to me to catch up with them. They, therefore, made an exception and agreed to accept direct Medicare consignment. But my bill for twenty-five outpatient radiation treatments and major surgery was $125,000. After third-party payments were credited, I had a balance of $7,000. But, Praise the Lord, there's more...

At the end of February, I called to set up a payment plan if all of my third-party payments had been credited. A customer service financial representative asked, 'Didn't you get a letter?' My mail goes to NC. I hadn't. They then asked if I remembered filing a request for financial assistance. I had; seven months prior. 'Your balance is '0.''

Thank you for your prayers. Look what God has done!

Love and Numbers 6:24-26 Blessings,
Trudy

# CHAPTER ELEVEN AND CHAPTER TWELVE

---

**The eleventh "P" is for *His Perfection* and
the twelfth "P" is for *His Performance*.**

Philippians 1:6:
"For I am confident of this very thing, that He who began a good work in
you will perfect it until the day of Christ Jesus."

---

I had tried to separate the eleventh "P," *His Perfection*, from the twelfth, *His Performance*, but found I could not. Consider Hebrews 1:3: "He is the radiance of His glory…" and "…the perfect representation of His being…" (Williams). It is because of who He is, that He has been able to do what He did, and what only He could do. In the Old Testament, the priest offered sacrifices repeatedly for sin, and once a year only entered the Holy of Holies, beyond the veil, into the Presence of God. Jesus, both as High Priest and our sacrifice, offered Himself as the perfect lamb of God, once for all, and "…when He had by Himself purged our sins…" is now "…sat down on the right hand of the Majesty on high…" (Hebrews 1:3, KJV). On the cross, He said, "It is finished" (John 19:30).

An inspirational writer summarizes this perfect work in these words:

> Because man's best efforts to reclaim and restore himself in the presence of an incredibly holy, righteous, and loving God fall far short, he is incapable of his own redemption. God Himself had to intervene on our behalf. He chose to become the supreme Substitute, who alone could atone for our misconduct and expiate our sins.
>
> This He did in the person of His own Son, Jesus Christ, the Savior of the world. He is *the Word, the very visible expression of the invisible God.* This 'God in the flesh' came to live, move, serve, and die amongst us—to be resurrected and return to His former glory.
>
> The 'perfect doing' and the 'perfect dying' of God in Christ, because it was that of the *Infinite One Himself,* suffices for all men of all time, be there billions upon billions of human beings.[1]

And Spurgeon:

> "Thou art fairer than the children of men."
> —Psalm 45:2

The entire person of Jesus is but as one gem, and His life is all along but one impression of the seal. He is altogether complete; not only in His several parts, but as a gracious all-glorious whole. His character is not a mass of fair colours mixed confusedly, nor a heap of precious stones laid carelessly one upon another; He is a picture of beauty and a breastplate of glory. In Him, all the 'things of good repute' are in their proper places, and assist in adorning each other. Not one feature in His glorious person attracts attention at the expense of others; but He is perfectly and altogether lovely.

Oh, Jesus! Thy power, Thy grace, Thy justice, Thy tenderness, Thy truth, Thy majesty, and Thine immutability make up such a man, or rather such a God-man, as neither heaven nor earth hath seen elsewhere. Thy infancy, Thy eternity, Thy sufferings, Thy triumphs, Thy death, and Thine immortality, are all woven in one gorgeous tapestry, without seam or rent. Thou art music without discord; Thou art many, and yet not divided; Thou art all things, and yet not diverse. As all the colours blend into one resplendent rainbow, so all the glories of heaven and earth meet in Thee, and unite so wondrously, that there is none like Thee in all things; nay, if all the virtues of the most excellent were bound in one bundle, they could not rival Thee, Thou mirror of all perfection. Thou hast been anointed with the holy oil of myrrh and cassia, which Thy God hath reserved for Thee alone; and as for Thy fragrance, it is as the holy perfume, the like of which none other can ever mingle, even with the art of the apothecary; each spice is fragrant, but the compound is divine.

> Oh, sacred symmetry! oh, rare connection
> Of many perfects, to make one perfection!
> Oh, heavenly music, where all parts do meet
> In one sweet strain, to make one perfect sweet![2]

John, Chapter 17, titled "The High Priestly Prayer," verse 4 says, "I glorified Thee on the earth, having accomplished the work which Thou hast given me to do." Jesus' going from His eternal home in glory with the Father to earth, accomplished the redemption of man, the eternal peace between God and man, the Father's purpose and plan. Jesus' life is a study of the purpose, the plan, the preparation, the provision, the presence, the promise, the peace, the power, the protection, the prosperity, the perfection, the performance, and the prayer of God in one man, one God-man. My going, your going, can be that same fulfillment of the Father's will in our lives.

And because of His perfect performance my, your, healing is completed.

Your Scripture Memory Verse is Isaiah 53:4-5:

"Surely he hath borne our griefs, and carried our sorrows: yet we did esteem him stricken, smitten of God, and afflicted. 5 But he was wounded for our transgressions, he was bruised for our iniquities: the chastisement of our peace was upon him; and with his stripes we are healed" (KJV).

Lastly, let's look at *His Prayer*, Chapter Thirteen.

# CHAPTER THIRTEEN

## The thirteenth "P" is for *His Prayer*.

Matthew 21:21-22 (KJV):
"Jesus answered and said unto them, 'Verily I say unto you, If ye have faith, and doubt not, ye shall not only do this which is done to the fig tree, but also if ye shall say unto this mountain, Be thou removed, and be thou cast into the sea; it shall be done. 22 And all things, whatsoever ye shall ask in prayer, believing, ye shall receive.'"

"Whatever you ask *in My name*, that will I do, so that the Father may be glorified in the Son. 14 If you ask Me anything in My name, I will do it" (John 14:13-14, emphasis mine).

What is prayer? I have heard many definitions. A familiar one is "talking to God." Prayer, as defined as "talking to God" is first mentioned in Genesis 3:8-11:

"They heard the sound of the Lord God walking in the garden in the cool of the day, and the man and his wife hid themselves from the presence of the Lord God among the trees of the garden. 9 Then the Lord God called to the man, and said to him, 'Where are you?' 10 He said, 'I heard the sound of You in the garden, and I was afraid because I was naked; so I hid myself.'"

This continues as a two-way conversation involving talking and listening.

Others have defined prayer by breaking it down into components, for example, praise, petition, thanksgiving; or types, private, corporate, intercessory. What is your definition?

_____

_____

One of my favorites comes from Christian author, Jan Karon. In *The Mitford Bedside Companion,* she defines prayer: "Calling home." We all know our home phone number. And to an empty-nester like me, those calls are never too frequent. I have also heard a certain Scripture reference referred to as "God's phone number." It's Jeremiah 33:3: "Call to Me and I will answer you..." Reminiscent of "Whosoever will call upon the name of the Lord will be saved" (Romans 10:13).

But I think my all-time favorite is from Experiencing God: "Prayer is a relationship, not a religious activity."[1]

If we have accepted Jesus as Lord and Savior, we are "adopted" into God's family, the trinity: The Father, the Son, Jesus, and the Holy Spirit. God as Father is now introduced by Jesus as Daddy, "Abba" (Luke 11:2). Jesus is now our brother. And we, also His Bride; He, Christ, our Bridegroom. Which even deepens our relationship with Father. He now is also Father-in-law. And the Holy Spirit, the Helper, the Counselor, the Comforter (John 15:26), abiding within us, is said to cry out with groanings too deep for words when we don't know how to pray (Romans 8:26).

Jesus' disciples, recognizing their need to know how to pray came to Jesus, the Teacher, and asked Him to teach them, as John the Baptist had his disciples.

Luke 11:1-4:

It happened that while Jesus was praying in a certain place, after He had finished, one of His disciples said to Him, 'Lord, teach us to pray just as John also taught his disciples.' 2 And He said to them, 'When you pray, say: Father, hallowed be Your name. Your kingdom come. 3 Give us each day our daily bread. 4 And forgive us our sins, For we ourselves also forgive everyone who is indebted to us. And lead us not into temptation.'

Outline the processes, in this model prayer Jesus prayed in Luke 11:

(1) Acknowledging who God is, verse 2.

_____

_____

(2) Praise, verse 2 (Hallowing him).

_____

_____

Matthew 6:10 adds "On earth as it is in heaven" (aligning with Heaven.)

(3) Petition, verse 3.

_____

_____

(4) (Conditional on) Forgiveness, verse 4.

_____

_____

(5) Protection from evil, verse 4.

_____

Matthew 6:13 (NKJV) adds "…but deliver us from the evil one."

> This prayer begins where all true prayer must commence, with the spirit of *adoption,* 'Our Father.' There is no acceptable prayer until we can say, 'I will arise, and go unto my Father.' This child-like spirit soon perceives the grandeur of the Father 'in heaven,' and ascends to *devout adoration,* 'Hallowed be Thy name.' The child lisping, 'Abba, Father,' grows into the cherub crying, 'Holy, Holy, Holy.' There is but a step from rapturous worship to the *glowing missionary spirit,* which is a sure outgrowth of filial love and reverent adoration—'Thy kingdom come, Thy will be done on earth as it is in heaven.'[2]

Dear reader, do you know Him as Abba, Father?

If you have experienced father loss, early or even later in life, you may feel a sense of abandonment as I once did. I used to pray the Our Father, and when I got to the part "who art in heaven," I'd inadvertently add, "I wish you weren't so far away." It took intimacy, growing a relationship with Jesus through the Holy Spirit, to internalize "the Kingdom is at hand" and my Father that close, a hand distance away.

And in Matthew 6:5-8 Jesus' teaching continues:

> When you pray, you are not to be like the hypocrites; for they love to stand and pray in the synagogues and on the street corners so that they may be seen by men. Truly I say to you, they have their reward in full. 6 But you, when you pray, go into your inner room, close your door and pray to your Father who is in secret, and your Father who sees what is done in secret will reward you. 7 And when you are praying, do not use meaningless repetition as the Gentiles do, for they suppose that they will be heard for their many words. 8 So do not be like them; for your Father knows what you need before you ask Him.

Now compare Matthew 6:5-8 with Luke 11:5-10 in your favorite translation. In these passages regarding prayer, can you identify two principles outlined?

_____

_____

_____

_____

Here, I am comparing Matthew 6:6, which identified praying in secret, and Matthew 6:7, not using meaningless repetition, with Luke 11:5-8, illustrating praying persistently. Persistence prevails. Ask, seek, and you will find. Knock and the door shall be opened (Luke 11:9-13).

You, like me, may have thought of the Our Father as the Lord's prayer, but consider John 17, called His High Priestly Prayer. Jesus prayed here for me and for you. Listen to these words, late in His earthly ministry, the night before His passion began, when His mission was nearing completion.

## The High Priestly Prayer

Jesus spoke these things; and lifting up His eyes to heaven, He said, 'Father, the hour has come; glorify Your Son, that the Son may glorify You, 2 even as You gave Him authority over all flesh, that to all whom You have given Him, He may give eternal life. 3 This is eternal life, that they may know You, the only true God, and Jesus Christ whom You have sent. 4 I glorified You on the earth, having accomplished the work which You have given Me to do. 5 Now, Father, glorify Me together with Yourself, with the glory which I had with You before the world was.

6 I have manifested Your name to the men whom You gave Me out of the world; they were Yours and You gave them to Me, and they have kept Your word. 7 Now they have come to know that everything You have given Me is from You; 8 for the words which You gave Me I have given to them; and they received them and truly understood that I came forth from You, and they believed that You sent Me. 9 I ask on their behalf; I do not ask on behalf of the world, but of those whom You have given Me; for they are Yours; 10 and all things that are Mine are Yours, and Yours are Mine; and I have been glorified in them. 11 I am no longer in the world; and yet they themselves are in the world, and I come to You. Holy Father, keep them in Your name, the name which You have given Me, that they may be one even as We are. 12 While I was with them, I was keeping them in Your name which You have given Me; and I guarded them and not one of them perished but the son of perdition, so that the Scripture would be fulfilled.

## The Disciples in the World

13 But now I come to You; and these things I speak in the world so that they may have My joy made full in themselves. 14 I have given them Your word; and the world has hated them, because they are not of the world, even as I am not of the world. 15 I do not ask You to take them out of the world, but to keep them from the evil one. 16 They are not of the world, even as I am not of the world. 17 Sanctify them in the truth; Your word is truth. 18 As You sent Me into the world, I also have sent them into the world. 19 For their sakes I sanctify Myself, that they themselves also may be sanctified in truth.

20 I do not ask on behalf of these alone, but for those also who believe in Me through their word; 21 that they may all be one; even as You, Father, are in Me and I in You, that they also may be in Us, so that the world may believe that You sent Me.

## Their Future Glory

22 The glory which You have given Me I have given to them, that they may be one, just as We are one; 23 I in them and You in Me, that they may be perfected in unity, so that the world may know that You sent Me, and loved them, even as You have loved Me. 24 Father, I desire that they also, whom You have given Me, be with Me where I am, so that they may see My glory which You have given Me, for You loved Me before the foundation of the world.

25 O righteous Father, although the world has not known You, yet I have known You; and these have known that You sent Me; 26 and I have made Your name known to them, and will make it known, so that the love with which You loved Me may be in them, and I in them.'

What did Jesus ask the Father for in the following verses?

Verses 1, 5

_____

_____

Verse 11

_____

_____

Verse 15

_____

_____

Verse 17

_____

_____

Verses 20-21

_____

_____

Verse 24

_____

_____

We looked at Luke 11:2-4. Now read Matthew 6:1, 9-13, comparing it with John 17. What similarity did you find in Matthew 6:1 and John 17:1? And between John 17:15, 22, 24 and Matthew 6:13?

_____

_____

_____

_____

Scripture records what Jesus told us to ask for.

- Ask the Lord to teach you how to pray. His disciples asked (Luke 11:1-4).
- Ask for the Holy Spirit (Luke 11:13). And when you receive Him, use your new prayer language. "With all prayer and petition pray at all times in the Spirit…" (Ephesians 6:18). And Romans 8:26-27 says:

"In the same way the Spirit also helps our weakness; for we do not know how to pray as we should, but the Spirit Himself intercedes for us with groanings too deep for words; 27 and He who searches the hearts knows what the mind of the Spirit is, because He intercedes for the saints according to the will of God."

John 14:16-17:
"I will ask the Father, and He will give you another Helper, that He may be with you forever; 17 that is the Spirit of truth, whom the world cannot receive, because it does not see Him or know Him, but you know Him because He abides with you and will be in you."

- And from the Old Testament, from the prophet Jeremiah 6:16 ask guidance:

"Thus says the Lord,
'Stand by the ways and see and ask for the ancient paths,
Where the good way is, and walk in it;
And you will find rest for your souls.'"

- And from Psalm 2:8, for the Gospel's sake, ask for your inheritance:

"Ask of Me, and I will surely give the nations as Your inheritance,
And the very ends of the earth as Your possession."

- Ask for a mantle(s) fallen to the earth (2 Kings 2).
- Ask to love Him more than anything (Matthew 22:37).
- And yes, ask for healing. But…also consider what Henry Blackaby writes in Experiencing God:

Have you ever prayed for one thing and got another? I have. Then some dear soul would say, 'God is trying to get you to persist. Keep on praying until you get what you want.' During one of those times I kept asking God in one direction, and I kept getting something else.

In the middle of that experience, I started reading from the second chapter of Mark in my quiet time. That is the story of the four men who brought their crippled friend to Jesus to be healed. Because of the crowd, they opened a hole in the roof and let the man down in front of Jesus. Jesus said, 'Son, your sins are forgiven' (Mark 2:5).

I started to read on, but I sensed that the Spirit of God said, 'Henry, did you see that?' I went back and began to meditate on that Scripture. Under the guiding, teaching ministry of the Holy Spirit, I began to see a wonderful truth. The four men were asking Jesus to heal the man, but Jesus forgave the man's sins. Why? They asked for one thing, and Jesus gave another! This man and his friends asked for a particular gift, but Jesus wanted to make the man a child of God so he could inherit everything!

I found myself weeping before God and saying: 'Oh, God, if I ever give you a request and You have more to give me than I'm asking, cancel my request!'[3]

An example of God's *more*:

1 Kings 3:5-14:
In Gibeon the Lord appeared to Solomon in a dream at night; and God said, 'Ask what you wish me to give you.'

Solomon's Prayer
6 Then Solomon said, 'You have shown great lovingkindness to Your servant David my father, according as he walked before You in truth and righteousness and uprightness of heart toward You; and You have reserved for him this great lovingkindness, that You have given him a son to sit on his throne, as it is this day. 7 Now, O Lord my God, You have made Your servant king in place of my father David, yet I am but a little child; I do not know how to go out or come in. 8 Your servant is in the midst of Your people which You have chosen, a great people who are too many to be numbered or counted. 9 So give Your servant an understanding heart to judge Your people to discern between good and evil. For who is able to judge this great people of Yours?'

God's Answer
10 It was pleasing in the sight of the Lord that Solomon had asked this thing. 11 God said to him, 'Because you have asked this thing and have not asked for yourself long life, nor have asked riches for yourself, nor have you asked for the life of your enemies, but have asked for yourself discernment to understand justice, 12 behold, I have done according to your words. Behold, I have given you a wise and discerning heart, so that there has been no one like you before you, nor shall one like you arise after you. 13 I have also given you what you have not asked, both riches and honor, so that there will not be any among the kings like you all your days. 14 If you walk in My ways, keeping My statutes and commandments, as your father David walked, then I will prolong your days.'

The Book of Psalms is one of my favorite books of the Bible. King David, described by God "...as a man after His own heart," (1 Samuel 13:14, Acts 13:22), is credited with most of its authorship, and it chronicles the hopes and joys and fears and struggles of his entire life. I previously mentioned Bible teacher Beth Moore. In *Stepping Up, a Journey through the Psalms of Ascent*, Beth takes the reader through Psalms 120-134. According to the Talmud, the collection of ancient Rabbinical writings guiding orthodox Judaism, each of these Psalms is connected to one of the fifteen steps of the temple, ascended by pilgrims coming to celebrate the Feasts in Jerusalem.[4] It is a study on praying the Psalms, and in it, Beth challenges the reader to write one's own version. If dated, it is an amazing diary, chronicling our very life. Once I got over my fear of changing one dot or letter of the word, I realized it was pragmatically teaching me how to pray, talking to God, bringing my life concerns, my church, and my city.

Let's try it. You can choose any Psalm. In my morning devotions today, I chose Psalm 136, with so much to be, and to learn to be grateful for, a Psalm of thanksgiving. It has twenty-six verses, and each end in *"His faithful love endures forever."* Read the Psalm first.

Psalm 136:
Give thanks to the Lord, for he is good!
His faithful love endures forever.
2 Give thanks to the God of gods.
His faithful love endures forever.
3 Give thanks to the Lord of lords.
His faithful love endures forever.
4 Give thanks to him who alone does mighty miracles.
His faithful love endures forever.
5 Give thanks to him who made the heavens so skillfully.
His faithful love endures forever.
6 Give thanks to him who placed the earth among the waters.
His faithful love endures forever.
7 Give thanks to him who made the heavenly lights
His faithful love endures forever.
8 The sun to rule the day,
His faithful love endures forever.
9 And the moon and stars to rule the night.
His faithful love endures forever.
10 Give thanks to him who killed the firstborn of Egypt.
His faithful love endures forever.
11 He brought Israel out of Egypt.
His faithful love endures forever.
12 He acted with a strong hand and powerful arm.
His faithful love endures forever.
13 Give thanks to him who parted the Red Sea.
His faithful love endures forever.
14 He led Israel safely through,
His faithful love endures forever.
15 But he hurled Pharaoh and his army into the Red Sea.
His faithful love endures forever.
16 Give thanks to him who led his people through the wilderness.
His faithful love endures forever.
17 Give thanks to him who struck down mighty kings.
His faithful love endures forever.
18 He killed powerful kings—
His faithful love endures forever.
19 Sihon king of the Amorites,
His faithful love endures forever.
20 And Og king of Bashan.
His faithful love endures forever.
21 God gave the land of these kings as an inheritance—
His faithful love endures forever.
22 A special possession to his servant Israel.
His faithful love endures forever.
23 He remembered us in our weakness.

His faithful love endures forever.
24 He saved us from our enemies.
His faithful love endures forever.
25 He gives food to every living thing.
His faithful love endures forever.
26 Give thanks to the God of heaven.
His faithful love endures forever
(New Living Translation).

Next, write your own entries. If you add even one a day you have started a process of learning to pray the Psalms.

Your Psalm 136
A Psalm of Thanksgiving

1 Give thanks to the Lord, for

_____

_____

*His faithful love endures forever.*

2 Give thanks

_____

_____

*His faithful love endures forever.*

3 Give thanks

_____

_____

*His faithful love endures forever.*

4 Give thanks to the Lord

_____

_____

*His faithful love endures forever.*

5 Give thanks

_____

*His faithful love endures forever.*

6 Give thanks

_____

_____

*His faithful love endures forever.*

7 Give thanks to the Lord

_____

_____

*His faithful love endures forever.*

8 Give thanks

_____

_____

*His faithful love endures forever.*

9 Give thanks

_____

_____

*His faithful love endures forever.*

10 Give thanks to the Lord

_____

_____

*His faithful love endures forever.*

11 Give thanks

_____

_____

*His faithful love endures forever.*

12 Give thanks

_____

_____

*His faithful love endures forever.*

13 Give thanks to the Lord

_____

_____

*His faithful love endures forever.*

14 Give thanks

_____

_____

*His faithful love endures forever.*

15 Give thanks

_____

_____

*His faithful love endures forever.*

16 Give thanks to the Lord

_____

_____

*His faithful love endures forever.*

17 Give thanks

_____

_____

*His faithful love endures forever.*

18 Give thanks

_____

_____

*His faithful love endures forever.*

19 Give thanks to the Lord

_____

_____

*His faithful love endures forever.*

20 Gives thanks

_____

_____

*His faithful love endures forever.*

21 Give thanks

_____

_____

*His faithful love endures forever.*

22 Give thanks

_____

_____

*His faithful love endures forever.*

23 Give thanks to the Lord

_____

_____

*His faithful love endures forever.*

24 Give thanks

_____

_____

*His faithful love endures forever.*

25 Give thanks

_____

_____

*His faithful love endures forever.*

26 Give thanks to the Lord

_____

_____

*His faithful love endures forever.*

Do you know the Bible story of Elijah's cloud the size of a man's hand? I see it now as a type or vision for our healing. In this story, the prophet has exercised authority (*exousia*) on God's directive that there would be no rain in Israel.

1 Kings 17:1; 18:1-2, 41-46:

Elijah was a prophet from the town of Tishbe in Gilead. He said to King Ahab, 'I serve the Lord, the God of Israel. By his power, I promise that no dew or rain will fall for the next few years. The rain will fall only when I command it to fall'…

18:1 During the third year that no rain fell, the Lord said to Elijah, 'Go meet with King Ahab, and I will make it rain.' 2 So Elijah went to meet with Ahab…

41 Then Elijah said to King Ahab, 'Now go eat and drink. A heavy rain is coming.' 42 So King Ahab went to eat. At the same time Elijah climbed to the top of Mount Carmel. At the top of the mountain Elijah bent down. He put his head between his knees. 43 Then Elijah said to his servant, 'Go up higher and look toward the sea.' The servant went and looked. He came back and said, 'I saw nothing.' Elijah told him to go look again. This happened seven times. 44 The seventh time, the servant came back and said, 'I saw a small cloud the size of a man's fist that was coming in from the sea.' Elijah told the servant, 'Go to tell King Ahab to get his chariot ready and go home now. If he does not leave now, the rain will stop him.'

45 After a short time the sky was covered with dark clouds. The wind began to blow, and a heavy rain began to fall. Ahab got in his chariot and started back to Jezreel. 46 The power of the Lord came to Elijah. He used his belt to hold up the bottom of his robe away from his feet. Then he ran ahead of King Ahab all the way to Jezreel (ERV).

Where is your cloudless sky? What do you need to see first in the spiritual, to birth in the natural? Healing for yourself or a loved one? Elijah was persistent: no cloud. He went back…again and again, and prayed.

How many times did Elijah pray? _____ How persistent are you?

Remember James 5:13-18:

> Is anyone among you suffering? Let him pray. Is anyone cheerful? Let him sing psalms. 14 Is anyone among you sick? Let him call for the elders of the church, and let them pray over him, anointing him with oil in the name of the Lord. 15 *And the prayer of faith will save the sick*, and the Lord will raise him up. And if he has committed sins, he will be forgiven. 16 Confess your trespasses to one another, and pray for one another, that you may be healed. *The effective, fervent prayer of a righteous man avails much.* 17 Elijah was a man with a nature like ours, and he prayed earnestly that it would not rain; and it did not rain on the land for three years and six months. 18 And he prayed again, and the heaven gave rain, and the earth produced its fruit (NKJV, emphasis mine).

The story James 5 references is 1 Kings 17:1; 18:1-2, 45-46 we studied.

After the brook had dried up, after the story of the provision of a widow, and three years of famine later, Elijah appears before Ahab and prophesies rain.

> 2 Samuel 22:30: "For by you I can run against a troop, and by my God I can leap over a wall" (ESV).

In your cancer battle, God gives strength to the weak, the weary.

> "And soon the sky was black with clouds. A heavy wind brought a terrific rainstorm, and Ahab left quickly for Jezreel. 46 Then the Lord gave special strength to Elijah. He tucked his cloak into his belt and ran ahead of Ahab's chariot all the way to the entrance of Jezreel" (1 Kings 18:45, New Living Translation).

In warfare, remember to tuck your garment into your belt of Truth as we studied in Chapter Nine. Each day is a gift from God to be savored.

"Each morning is a sort of resurrection…as every morning brings to us, in fact, a resurrection from what might have been our tomb and delivers us from the image of death which through the night we wore, it ought to be saluted with thanksgiving."[5]

And each evening we need to be mindful of the providence, the protection and provision of God that we have experienced that day and rejoice with gratitude.

*My Story*

A book, *The Battle Plan for Prayer,*[6] from the movie *War Room*, was gifted to me when I was scheduled for intercessory prayer. I had asked for a Stephen minister to be assigned to me my short-term treatment stay in Florida but one was not available. But the couple who coordinated that ministry of helps scheduled me for intercession both at the Church of Eleven22 and the Prayer Room previously mentioned (*My Story*, Chapter Eight), even driving me to the location. I had seen the movie *War Room*, a model of intercession changing lives, and the book was a war manual placed in my hands for the on-going battles.

Corporate prayer is powerful. The most important thing I raised in my YWAM faith challenge as mentioned in *My Story*, were intercessors, prayer warriors to hold my head and hands up. In the corporate Prayer Room in Jacksonville before my surgery, one had been in intercession three hours that morning for me, a yet unknown stranger, yet sister in Christ Jesus, believing for a miracle of God's healing, transforming love.

"Prayer is always the preface to blessing. It goes before the blessing as the blessing's shadow."[7] And corporate prayer reflects the very heart of the Trinity, Father, Son, and Holy Spirit. Matthew 18:19-20: "...if two of you agree on earth about anything that they may ask, it shall be done for them by My Father who is in heaven. 20 For where two or three have gathered together in My name, I am there in their midst." And Acts 2:1-2: "...they were all with one accord in one place" (NKJV), followed by the manifestation of tongues of fire, *dunamis* power like the burning bush (Exodus 3:2), and the pillar that led the Israelites by night (Exodus 13:21). "For our God is a consuming fire" (Hebrews 12:29, KJV).

In John 17, Jesus prayed not for His Twelve alone, but for you and me: "...those who believe in Me through their word..." What prayer partners we have, Jesus Himself and the Holy Spirit (Romans 8:26). This final "P," *Prayer*, should be the alpha and the omega, the beginning, and the ending of our "Going."

The words of a song echo through my mind, "...*All the children sit around the Father's table...who will go into the Father's vineyard?*" Remember as you and your loved ones go through a cancer battle, His Purpose, His Plan, His Preparation, His Provision, His Presence, His Promises, His Peace, His Power, His Protection, His Prosperity, His Perfection, His Performance, and His Prayer go with you.

Will you "*Go*"? "Go" into your Father's vineyard? Will you finish the work He's given you to do?

R. S. V. P.

---

# CHAPTER FOURTEEN

# Epilogue

Pastor Kevin Taylor recently asked if I'm going to include how to maintain one's healing in this manuscript. Yes, I am, and I must. Though I had won the war on cancer, its aftermath continued in battles for my health as my body adjusted to what we in the medical profession label "status post," the new normal.

But after I shared this with my twin sons, David and Jonathan, their identical response unsettled me. "Mom, if you've found a cure for cancer, you have a *New York Times Best Seller*." I hadn't. All my certainties became uncertain in that light. According to the National Cancer Institute, there are more than one hundred types of cancer, some named for the organs and tissues where they form, others for the types of cells. And then they are staged in progression, from in situ (localized) to metastatic (change in location).

But…God is not limited by any of the above. *Cancer Overcomers: Gold Refined by Fire* has focused on the spirit of man thus far. But man is a tripartite being. Allow me now to include some thoughts on man's body and soul for you to consider.

According to new definitions, you, if you've been diagnosed with cancer and are alive, are a cancer survivor. I like that. Contemplate that reality. *"Survivor."* That thought energizes and empowers me.

But if even a new vehicle requires documented records of periodic maintenance to keep the manufacturer's warranty in effect, so do we. Second Corinthians 5:17-18 says, "Therefore, if anyone is in Christ, he is a new creation. The old has passed away; behold, the new has come…" (ESV). Or in the Complete Jewish Bible, it reads, "—the old has passed; look, what has come is fresh and new! And it is all from God." You *are* a new creation in Christ Jesus. Old things *have* passed away. "The Book" from your Manufacturer is His Word, the Bible. So, let's revisit some of the thirteen "P's" again to see His warranty requirements.

*His Purpose* as outlined in Chapter One was "…that I may know Him…" (Philippians 3:10). That relationship, above all others, requires periodic maintenance. The Manufacturer recommends daily prayer, reading His word regularly, and "…the children's bread," (Matthew 15:26, healing), Holy Communion, for your continuing wholeness.

If you are new to Bible reading, you may want to start with the New Testament, the gospels (glad tidings), Matthew, Mark, Luke, and John. You will see there the ministry of Jesus, His healing compassion that will grow your faith. Remember the suggestion of starting/keeping a healing journal. Journal there your prayer requests and answered prayers as well.

Do you have a church fellowship? Don't walk this path alone. My intercessors, my Aaron and Hur (Exodus 17:12), raised my head and my hands when I was weak.

If God's *Purpose* is that we know Him, what is yours? And if you have lost *your* purpose and direction in life, your lifeline to live, ask another question. How? Abruptly with a change in life's course or slowly like the tide eroding a beach over time? Did you or a loved one's cancer come at a time, like mine, of great transitions? Empty nest? Retirement? Losses? If so, your purpose may need some adjustment. If you defined your life as a mom, you can still be a role model. First, you may have to grieve the losses once you've identified them.

*The Purpose Driven Life* outlines five purposes for your life: (1) You were planned for God's pleasure; (2) You were formed for God's family; (3) You were created to become like Christ; (4) You were shaped for serving God; and (5) You were made for a mission.[1] If you have not done so already, ask God to reveal by His Holy Spirit your mission for your life. A mission from the Latin root means "sending." Remember John 3:16? God "sent" His only Son into the world. Our ministry is our gift to believers, but our mission, our service to unbelievers.[2]

> "Jesus clearly understood his life mission on earth. At age twelve He said, 'I must be about My Father's business,' and twenty-one years later, dying on the cross, He said, 'It is finished.' Like bookends, these two statements frame a well-lived, purpose-driven life. Jesus completed the mission the Father gave Him."[3]

We come to know Him, our Father who art in heaven, and who we are in Him. Then "…we might say that we were sent here to learn how to be sons of God, and daughters of God, before anything else…Being issues into Doing."[4]

Chapter Two was *His Preparation*. In the spirit realm, you can prepare for battle(s), even cancer. Salvation (*sozo*) is the complete health of body, soul, and spirit. And the Baptism of the Holy Spirit is your entrance into *dunamis* power.

But in the natural, for me, the diagnosis of cancer came as a surprise, off my radar entirely. I had spent years of my life, it seemed, building my immune system. "One theory of cancer called the 'surveillance theory,' says that we in fact get and defeat cancer many times during our lives. The body develops abnormal cells, but the immune system destroys them before they multiply enough to be dangerous. But if our immune system is depleted by stress, our defenses fail and a cancer develops."[5]

A wise person once said, "An ounce of prevention is worth a pound of cure." Can we apply this to cancer? Possibly. Look back over your life to the eighteen months preceding the cancer diagnosis. Chronicle those events in your healing journal. How high was your stress then? If you need a model scale, I've used the Holmes-Rahe Stress Inventory.[6] How high is your stress level now? What steps can you take to reduce it if necessary? And how do you respond to stress? If you're not sure, look at the family role models in your life. Do they, possibly you also, internalize stress (keep feelings in, prone to migraine headaches) or externalize (aggressive stress responder, Type A personality)? Internalizers, older research has shown, are cancer prone; externalizers, heart disease prone. Do you have a support person/system in place? If not, what steps can you take now to build or re-build one? Please journal your thoughts.

But make the first question you answer in your journal be, "Do you want to live?" Research has shown that this is the single most significant question in your cancer battle, predictive of the outcome. And "… Have I lived enough? Have I loved enough?" are questions from the writer John Steinbeck, quoted in *The Healing Heart*.[7] My answer to Steinbeck's was a definite, "*No.*" Did you or your loved one feel like this also?

Your "going," as outlined in *His Plan*, Chapter Three, is part of a shared mission. But yours is also unique and specific. What are your gifts and talents? What are the God-given desires He has placed in your heart? They are clues to discover or redefine your mission during your healing journey.

Remember, as part of your "going," you may have to forgive those who have hurt you or you've hurt, reconciling some relationships along the way. Healing of body, soul, and spirit is a process, an on-going process. His forgiveness is contingent on ours (Luke 11:4).

In 1 Kings 17:7 we read the prophet Elijah declared to wicked King Ahab that there would be no dew or rain in Israel for the next few years except by his word. Then he ran and hid. For a season, God miraculously sustained Elijah with water from a brook and bread and meat brought to him faithfully, morning and evening, by ravens. Can you imagine this supernatural provision? But then...the brook dried up. What is your brook? Has it, too, dried up? My brook can be anything other than God Himself I lean on: a relationship, a job, and yes, even my health, my natural strength. And what do I do when my brook dries up? What did Elijah do? For the rest of the story, review 1 Kings 17 in your favorite Bible translation. Maintaining your healing may be contingent on your answer(s).

An example of relying on human strength, King David grieved the Lord by taking a census of Israel, numbering the fighting men throughout the tribes from Dan to Beersheba,

> The prophet Gad, David's seer, came to him with the word of the Lord, giving David three choices of punishment: three years of famine, three months of fleeing while his enemies pursued him, or three days of plague. David chose to fall into the hands of the Lord, not men. Thus, a plague broke out killing 70,000. As it approached Jerusalem, the Lord was grieved and declared, "Enough! Withdraw your hand," to the angel afflicting the people. Where the plague stopped was the threshing floor of Araunah the Jebusite. The angel spoke again to David through the prophet Gad, "Go up and build an altar there on the threshing floor of Araunah the Jebusite" (2 Samuel 24).

Those verses stopped me completely. Where has my/your cancer plague stopped? What does it mean to build an altar there? And in 2 Samuel 24:24, David says, "I will not sacrifice to the Lord my God burnt offerings that cost me nothing." What has cancer cost you? I mean much more than financially, though that is undeniably a part.

Remember in Chapter Four, *His Provision*, Abraham "altared" his Isaac. There too, on Moriah, the very threshing floor of Araunah the Jebusite, Solomon laid the foundation for the temple delegated by the Lord through David his father (2 Chronicles 3:1, NIV). What can you now bring to the altar? A thanksgiving offering (Jeremiah 33:11; Amos 4:5). In the New Testament story of the healing of ten lepers in the Complete Jewish Bible, Jesus asked the one who came back to thank Him, "Weren't ten cleansed? Where are the other nine? Was no one found coming back to give glory to God except this foreigner?" (Luke 17:17-18)

Proverbs 17:22 says: "Happiness is good medicine, but sorrow is a disease" (ERV). A thankful heart is a joyful heart. Are you keeping up gratitude entries in your healing journal?

Chapter Five was *His Peace*. When I chose a cancer center, I didn't see the big picture, a five-year follow-up. It implied healing may not be an instantaneous event, but a process. But I had come across a book with a message I could grab onto, *The Healing Journey*: "In the deepest sense, healing from cancer is healing your life...the message of cancer is always one of love." The Simonton Cancer Treatment Center advocates: "...Develop...a two-year plan...about changing your day-to-day routines in six areas over the next two years: (1) purpose in life; (2) play; (3) exercise; (4) social support; (5) nutrition; and (6) creative thinking."[8] They advise setting realistic, measurable goals in three-month increments. For example, exercise. You may have to start with bed or wheelchair ones as I did, having a five-minute standing tolerance after surgery. Physical therapy advanced me in a home program with a walker to outside terrain and walking in my apartment for ten minutes. Yes, baby steps. The hardest one has been learning to play again. That's still in process.

Healing of body, soul, and spirit is a process, an on-going process. Have you neglected or abused your body in any way, even nutritionally? The book, *Let Food Be Your Medicine*, by Don Colbert, M.D. comes to mind. Have you exposed yourself to carcinogens, i.e., nicotine, secondary smoke, environmental toxins? Cancer can be your personal 9/11, your 911 wake-up call for change(s). Your outcome(s) may be contingent on how you answer that call.

And creativity may need rekindling after the serious life-or-death struggle against cancer. Simonton graphs those six areas mentioned above in three-month intervals and suggests you go slowly, maybe to nine months at the start.

And if cancer has served the purpose of our making positive lifestyle changes over a period of time, do we need it anymore? Lifestyle changes can become a good habit.

In *Half Time, Changing Your Game Plan from Success to Significance,*[9] I read of the analogy of any sport divided into halves, like our early and later lives, and an invitation to do differently in the second half. Your "second half" can be life after cancer.

A native Pittsburgher, I watched an interview during half-time, *Football Night in America*, with Michele Tafoya interviewing James Conner, a survivor, status-post Hodgkin's lymphoma playing with the Pittsburgh Steelers. Conner says in the interview:

> You think you're healthy and you hear about someone having cancer, and you say a prayer for them and you go about your day. But, when it's with you, it never leaves… I've been in a dark place before. You start thinking things, and you learn how to control your mind and see how you can get the winning edge… With time. Prayer and time… Everything happened so fast. I'm thankful for everything. I wouldn't change anything. A lot of ups and downs like a roller coaster, but I would always focus on the positive.
>
> Then asked if he would change having to go through cancer and chemotherapy… No, not at all. It made me so grateful, and appreciative of everything. It's like a movie, almost, the way everything played out. So, no, I wouldn't change nothing. Everything was meant to be, and I'm a Pittsburgh Steeler, so, I'm happy.[10]

How has the experience of cancer changed you and /or your loved ones?

_____

_____

_____

What would you change about this experience if you could change anything?

_____

_____

_____

In 2 Kings 8:1-6, the story of the widow and Elisha, reads:

> Years before, Elisha had told the woman whose son he had brought to life, 'Leave here and go, you and your family, and live someplace else. God has ordered a famine in the land; it will last for seven years.' 2 The woman did what the Holy Man told her and left. She and her family lived as aliens in the country of Philistia for seven years. 3 Then, when the seven years were up, the woman and her family came back. She went directly to the king and asked for her home and farm. 4 The king was talking with Gehazi, servant to the Holy Man, saying, 'Tell me some stories of the great things Elisha did.' 5 It so happened that as he was telling the king the story of the dead person brought back to life, the woman whose son was brought to life showed up asking for her home and farm. Gehazi said, 'My master the king, this is the woman! And this is her son whom Elisha brought back to life!' 6 The king wanted to know all about it, and so she told him the story. The king assigned an officer to take care of her, saying, 'Make sure she gets everything back that's hers, plus all profits from the farm from the time she left until now' (The Message).

There is a seed of truth sown in this story, like so many of Jesus' parables; resurrection is followed by restoration and restitution. Store and apply that concept in your belief system of your expectations of Him following cancer.

In Chapter Eleven, we studied *His Perfection,* and in Chapter Twelve, *His Performance.* Remember, after four-hundred-thirty years of slavery in Egypt, in the Exodus after the celebration of the lamb, none were feeble or lame. God's restoration is a complete and finished work since Calvary. Isaiah 53:4-5 bears repeating:

> "Surely he hath borne our griefs, and carried our sorrows: yet we did esteem him stricken, smitten of God, and afflicted. 5 But he was wounded for our transgressions, he was bruised for our iniquities: the chastisement of our peace was upon him; and with his stripes we are healed" (KJV).

Chapter Thirteen addressed prayer. "Prayer is always the preface to blessing. It goes before the blessing as the blessing's shadow."[11] Pray in the name of Jesus.

> Acts 4:10,12: "...by the name of Jesus Christ the Nazarene...whom God raised from the dead—by this name this man stands here before you in good health...12 And there is salvation in no one else; for there is no other name under heaven that has been given among men by which we must be saved."

Corporate prayer reflects the very heart of the Trinity, Father, Son, and Holy Spirit. And historically, corporate prayer was followed by the manifestation of tongues of fire, (Acts 2) *dunamis* power like the burning bush (Exodus 3:2), and the pillar that led the Israelites by night (Exodus 13:21). How much more then we need to pray together for our brother's and sister's healing.

Do you have local access to healing prayer? Do you have a praying church? If not, there are national and international ministries and local TV and radio broadcasters that have pastors available to pray with you. There were chapels and chaplains available in my healing path. And some congregations have a Faith Community Nurse to walk alongside you as an advocate and ombudsman. And what would the effect be if one even prayed for themselves fifteen minutes a day, laying hands on the cancer site? For what prayer partners we have: Jesus seated at the right hand of the Father, living to make intercession for us, and the Holy Spirit, residing within us, allowing us to pray in unknown tongues when we do not know how to pray.

Our opening Scripture, Philippians 3:10 "…that I may know Him, and the power of His resurrection…," continues "and the fellowship of His sufferings…" I choked on that on first reading. But note that "the fellowship of His sufferings" is preceded by "the power of His resurrection" and followed by "…being conformed to His death; in order that I may attain to the resurrection from the dead."

Author and Bible teacher Henry Blackaby writes of his experience:

> When our only daughter was sixteen, the doctors told us she had cancer. We had to take her through chemotherapy and radiation. We suffered along with Carrie as we watched her experience the sickness that goes along with treatments. Some people face such an experience by blaming God and questioning why He doesn't love them anymore. Carrie's cancer treatments could have been a very devastating experience for us. Was God loving us still? Yes. Had His love changed? No, His love had not changed. At times I went before the Heavenly Father, and I saw behind my daughter the cross of Jesus Christ. I said, 'Father, don't ever let me look at circumstances and question your love for me. Your love for me was settled on the cross. That has never changed and will never change for me.' Our love relationship with the Heavenly Father sustained us through a very difficult time.[12]

I cried tonight during my chronological Bible study, reading 1 Kings 14:13. The prophet Ahijah nearly blind, was seeing in the Spirit the wife of Jeroboam, King of Israel, disguising herself to ask the outcome of her son's illness. Ahijah answers:

"He is the only one belonging to Jeroboam who will be buried, because he is the only one in the house of Jeroboam in whom the Lord, the God of Israel, has found anything good."

Can death be a blessing, a good gift, to preserve one from the days of evil ordained ahead? An answer to the age-old question: why the good die young? Can it be mercy, dear one, if you struggle with a cancer battle and lose? Paul says, "I fought the good fight. I ran the race." Will that be enough this side of heaven?

What if—what if—despite what you knew to do following your diagnosis, and did, your cancer has recurred at a primary or secondary site? Dear one, my heart goes out to you, and with it, my prayers again. If an initial diagnosis causes shock waves for up to three to six months,[14] then statistically, recurrence does also. But you, and I, are not a statistic, your diagnosis is. You do not have cancer. You are a patient "with…"

Sir William Osler, the father of bedside medicine has been quoted: "It is much more important to know what sort of patient has a disease than to know what sort of disease a patient has." You and I are precious and priceless and dearly loved by our heavenly Father. And you and I are becoming warriors, trained to defeat all the powers of darkness. Psalm 18:34 reads: "He trains my hands for war until my arms can bend a bow of bronze…" (CJB).

And the Bible verse that reminds me most what to do in darkness is Acts 16:25-26:

"But about midnight Paul and Silas were praying and singing hymns of praise to God, and the prisoners were listening to them; and suddenly there came a great earthquake, so that the foundations of the prison house were shaken; and immediately all the doors were opened and everyone's chains were unfastened."

"But about midnight…" At midnight, the night is very dark, the dawn far away. Are you there? And if, so, what are you to do? In Acts, Paul and Silas, though in prison and fettered, had the clarity of mind and Spirit, to know what to do: "…pray…and sing…" We've talked previously about building an altar and not offering God a sacrifice "…that would cost me nothing" in the words of King David. This may be the darkest hour, and the hardest sacrifice to offer God at this moment. But there is power in praise. The tribe of Judah, the praisers, went before Israel's army into battle. And the result, to the New Testament army of believers, Paul and Silas, was "…and suddenly there came a great earthquake, so that the foundations of the prison house were shaken; and immediately all the doors were opened and everyone's chains were unfastened."

In *The Meal That Heals*, Perry Stone also writes of what to do:

> Once God has wrought a healing for you, whether through the prayer of faith, a manifestation of the Spirit, or through Communion, He makes good His healing work, and your faith and obedience maintain a continual flow of life into your spirit, soul, and body. However, occasionally the enemy will counterattack, attempting to bring the very thing you were freed from back into your body. This is not Goliath, because that giant is dead. It may look the same, feel the same, and act the same, but Goliath has a brother. Lahmi [1 Chronicles 20:5] must be dealt with just as Goliath was dealt with.[14]

Remember from Psalm 139, the Presence Psalm, we studied earlier: "…darkness and light are alike to Thee" (Verse 12). So do the very things you did the first time that defeated your cancer Goliath. But if you have not yet asked God in His Sovereign wisdom to reveal the root of your cancer, do so. Put the ax to the root. In 2003, at a tent revival, I was prayed over. My sobbing was so intense, that the person who accompanied me said, "I never knew you had that much pain inside." And the minister prophesied, "They got it all." A puzzling word then, but to me, a nurse, it evoked reference to cancer. Did God allow me to store that word in my heart for twelve years? Was it referring to my yet unseen cancer, my mother's worst fear for my life after losing her firstborn son to a sarcoma (the cancer type I was diagnosed with, but his, of the lung)? The root, I've come to believe, was self-hatred, manifesting in life-long internalized anger, depression, and a battle with suicide ideation, compounded by losses. My healing, a process begun then, came in layers over the years. Cancer is a chance, perhaps a second chance, to be reconciled to God, yourself, and others.

Another cancer survivor writes:

> …more than nine months after surgery, I have 'recovered'—not recovered what I had, or who I was, before the call from Kathy in Dr. Russo's office changed my life. I do not think that will ever happen, and perhaps I no longer care. I'm not sure I *liked* that person nearly as much as I do the one that I am now, or the life I had then was as good as I thought it was. No, recovery comes, in the end, from the dawning realization that cancer was an *episode* in one's life, neither the end of it nor, more important, the whole of it.[15]

Of the cancer diagnosis I was given, I initially sensed, as told in *My Story*, the Holy Spirit weeping. How much more then can I believe Psalm 56:8:

> "You keep track of all my sorrows.
> You have collected all my tears in your bottle.
> You have recorded each one in your book"
> (New Living Translation).

Remember the story of Natalie Grant? Recently listening to KLOVE, I caught the end of another inspirational message: *Consider it a gift when God is your only option.*

When we are young, we feel invincible. But honestly, to face cancer, is to face the possibility of losing the battle, death. What is it that you believe about death?

_____

_____

_____

_____

Those friends and family who are comfortable with their mortality will likely be your closest allies. Others, because of their fears, will likely keep at a greater distance.

"Your eyes have seen my unformed substance;
And in Your book were all written
The days that were ordained for me,
When as yet there was not one of them"
(Psalm 139:16).

And perhaps more importantly than what you believe about death, what have you come to believe about life after death?

_____

_____

_____

_____

I believe in life everlasting, the gift I received when I accepted Jesus (John 3:16) and invited Him to be Lord of my life. I also believe that death is like the prodigal son(s) coming home to the Father. He is watching and waiting to welcome our homecoming with His open arms.

"Precious in the sight of the Lord is the death of His godly ones"
(Psalm 116:15).

"When they arrive at the gates of death,
God welcomes those who love him"
(Psalm 116:15, The Message).

"Even though I walk through the valley of the shadow of death,
I fear no evil, for You are with me...
6 Surely goodness and lovingkindness will follow me all the days of my life,

And I will dwell in the house of the Lord forever"
(Psalm 23:4, 6).

"He will wipe away every tear from their eyes, and death shall be no more, neither shall there
be mourning nor crying nor pain anymore, for the former things have passed away.
5 And he who was seated on the throne said, 'Behold, I am making all things new'"
(Revelation 21:4-5: ESV).

*******

In closing, dear reader, I want you to look with me at the Book of Revelation.

"And they overcame him because of the blood of the Lamb, and because of the word
of their Testimony, and they did not love their lives even to death" (Revelation 12:11).

We will study Chapters One through Three in your favorite version, the promises to The Overcomers.

## REVELATION

The book of Revelation is The Revelation of _____ _____ (Revelation 1:1).
Our study of the names of God which began with *Jeshua* (*the Lord saves*), ends here with Revelation 1:8: "I am the Alpha and the Omega," says the Lord God, "who is and who was and who is to come, the Almighty."

*Alpha* means

_____

_____

NT:1 "A (al'-fah); of Hebrew origin; the first letter of the alphabet; figuratively, only (from its use as a numeral) the first."[16]

*Omega* means

_____

_____

NT:5598 "omega (o'-meg-ah); the last letter of the Greek alphabet, i.e. (figuratively) the finality."[17]

Revelation 19:10: "For the testimony of Jesus is the spirit of prophecy."

What is a testimony?

_____

_____

From the Greek, NT:3141 "marturi/a (mar-too-ree'-ah); from NT:3144; evidence given (judicially or genitive case). KJV: record, report, testimony, witness."[18]

And how does that become prophecy?

NT:4393 "prophero (prof-er'-o); from NT:4253 and NT:5342; to bear forward, i.e., produce; NT:4394 propheteia (prof-ay-ti'-ah); from NT:4396 ('prophecy'); prediction (scriptural or other); from NT:4396; to foretell events, divine, speak under inspiration, exercise the prophetic office. KJV: bring forth; prophecy, prophesying."[19]

Bill Johnson, Bethel Church, says it means "Do it again."[20] When we testify of Jesus, what He's done for us, it starts a wave another can catch and ride in the spirit realm.

As the title of this book, *Cancer Overcomers*, suggests, there is much to understand about the process, the refining process, of becoming an overcomer. Revelation gives glimpses of this mystery and the rewards, fulfilled promises, that await the believer who overcomes. In the seven churches addressed we see this unfolding. Look up each verse and fill in the blanks. Check your answers with the answer key following.

(1) Message to Ephesus, Revelation 2:7: "To him who overcomes, _____

_____

_____

(2) Message to Smyrna, Revelation 2:11: "He who overcomes _____

_____

_____

(3) Message to Pergamum, Revelation 2:17: "To him who overcomes, to him I will give

_____

_____

(4) Message to Thyatira, Revelation 2:26-28: "He who overcomes, and he who keeps My deeds until the end

_____

_____

(5) Message to Sardis, Revelation 3:5-6: "He who overcomes _____

_____

_____

(6) Message to Philadelphia, Revelation 3:12-13: "He who overcomes, _____

_____

_____

(7) Message to Laodicea, Revelation 3:21: "He who overcomes, _____

_____

_____

Answer key:

(1) "…I will grant to eat of the tree of life which is in the Paradise of God."
(2) "…will not be hurt by the second death."
(3) "…some of the hidden manna, and I will give him a white stone, and a new name written on the stone which no one knows but he who receives it."
(4) "…to him I will give authority over the nations; 27 and he shall rule them with a rod of iron, as the vessels of the potter are broken to pieces, as I also have received authority from My Father; 28 and I will give him the morning star."
(5) "…will thus be clothed in white garments; and I will not erase his name from the book of life, and I will confess his name before My Father and before His angels."
(6) "…I will make him a pillar in the temple of My God, and he will not go out from it anymore; and I will write on him the name of My God, and the name of the city of My God, the new Jerusalem, which comes down out of heaven from My God, and My new name."
(7) "…I will grant to him to sit down with Me on My throne, as I also overcame and sat down with My Father on His throne."

The precious blood of Christ.
—1 Peter 1:19

Standing at the foot of the cross, we see hands, and feet, and side, all distilling crimson streams of precious blood. It is 'precious' because of its redeeming and atoning efficacy. By it the sins of Christ's people are atoned for; they are redeemed from under the law; they are reconciled to God, made one with Him. Christ's blood is also 'precious' in its cleansing power; it 'cleansed from all sin.' 'Though your sins be as scarlet, they shall be as white as snow.' Through Jesus' blood there is not a spot left upon any believer, no wrinkle nor any such thing remains. O precious blood, which makes us clean, removing the stains of abundant iniquity, and permitting us to stand accepted in the Beloved, notwithstanding the many ways in which we have rebelled against our God. The blood of Christ is likewise 'precious' in its preserving power. We are safe from the destroying angel under the sprinkled blood. Remember it is God's seeing the blood which is the true reason for our being spared. Here is comfort for us when the eye of faith is dim, for God's eye is still the same. The blood of Christ is 'precious' also in its sanctifying influence. The same blood which justifies by taking away sin, does in its after-action, quicken the new nature and lead it onward to subdue sin and to follow out the commands of God. There is no motive for holiness so great as that which streams from the veins of Jesus. And 'precious,' unspeakably precious, is this blood, because it has an overcoming power. It is written, 'They overcame through the blood of the Lamb.' How could they do otherwise? He who fights with the precious blood of Jesus, fights with a weapon which cannot know defeat. The blood of Jesus! sin dies at its presence, death ceases to be death: heaven's gates are opened. The blood of Jesus! we shall march on, conquering and to conquer, so long as we can trust its power![21]

In conclusion, we will look at the refining process itself. Revelation 3:15-21:

'I know your deeds, that you are neither cold nor hot; I wish that you were cold or hot. 16 So because you are lukewarm, and neither hot nor cold, I will spit you out of My mouth. 17 Because you say, I am rich, and have become wealthy, and have need of nothing, and you do not know that you are wretched and miserable and poor and blind and naked, 18 I advise you to *buy from Me gold refined by fire* so that you may become rich, and white garments so that you may clothe yourself, and that the shame of your nakedness will not be revealed; and eye salve to anoint your eyes so that you may see. 19 Those whom I love, I reprove and discipline; therefore be zealous and repent. 20 Behold, I stand at the door and knock; if anyone hears My voice and opens the door, I will come in to him and will dine with him, and he with Me' (Emphasis mine).

There is a cost, as the word *buy* implies. In Luke 14:28 we are advised to count the cost before building, and wisdom would add, before buying.

Robin McMillan, Senior Pastor, Queen City Church, Charlotte, North Carolina citing the story of Joseph (Genesis 37-50) writes:

"God is releasing new levels of anointing, colorful mantles He freely gives, but each one comes with a price."

But in, or coming into, or ending a cancer storm, the price is right. God gifted me with a mantle of revelation light to know who He is, and my authority (*exousia*) in Him, and the power (*dunamis*) of the Holy Spirit working through me. He taught my hands to war (Psalm 144:1). Beloved, Jesus Christ is the same yesterday, today, and forever (Hebrews 13:8).

My testimony can be the spirit of prophecy in your life as you apply this teaching and pray for yourself and others.

Thank you for accompanying me on my journey. My testimony continues, and yours is in the process of being written.

Blessings and peace for the journey,
Your sister in Christ, Trudy

24 "The Lord bless you, and keep you;
25 The Lord make His face shine on you,
And be gracious to you;
26 The Lord lift up His countenance on you,
And give you peace.
27 So they shall invoke My name on the sons of Israel, and I then will bless them"
(Numbers 6:24-26).

"Be exalted, O God, above the heavens;
let your glory be over all the earth."
(Psalm 57:11).

# BEHIND THE SCENES

I want to share with you how *Cancer Overcomers, Book One,* was birthed. There were thirteen moves between YWAM, Kona, Hawaii and my return to Surfside Beach, to a friend's condo, where I was house-sitting, a mile from the beach.

Thus, I had come full circle. But I needed some stability in my life to continue my healing process, now well underway. I found rentals pricey on a fixed social security income, but could I afford or qualify for a mortgage? With the clearing of my medical debt, as told in *My Story,* I was emboldened to contact a lender. Miraculously, I qualified for a U.S.D.A. loan, meaning rural agricultural, with one hundred percent financing, no money down. A true answer to prayer. A property search ensued, first in Horry, Georgetown, and Brunswick counties, then Lancaster, York, and Chester, South Carolina. The lot seemed to fall on Chester, SC, thirty minutes from my daughter. I closed on a 1930 vintage house, fully remodeled and I moved.

But at points during my first year's occupancy, I questioned what I was doing in Chester, SC, as putting down new roots was a slow process. The Father's House, the church I attended at the beach before moving, had told me of prophetic training a young pastor had received at a church in Chester and to look up the pastor when I got there. In a GodStop as described in this manuscript, a back-fence neighbor invited me to her church, Chester Freedom Ministries, the following Sunday. I then did an internet search by name for the previously recommended pastor. They turned out to be the same person.

Later that summer, I attended a Bible study there, "Acts Twenty-nine, Acts of the Holy Spirit." One night this Pastor, Steve Bishop, described the cancer battle of a man loved by that congregation who had died in his recurrent battles. He shared that this man, Gene Underwood, had wanted to write a guide through cancer and would never get to do it now. He added, "I'm not a writer. I've never had cancer, and I never want that experience. So, I'll not be the one to finish what Gene started." My reaction while I was seated in that class was, "I'm a writer. I've had cancer," but dismissed the thought immediately. That next morning, about 4:15 a.m., I found myself wide-awake with the startling thought revisited, "I'm a writer. I've had cancer," and the unction of the Holy Spirit all over those words, that I sensed was a commissioning to write. From there, *Cancer Overcomers: Gold Refined by Fire, The Thirteen P's* was birthed, the Holy Spirit moving again, Acts Twenty-nine.

# NOTES

## Prologue

[1] Matthew 19: 21-22, story of the rich young ruler who said, "*No*."

[2] Rick Joyner, *The Prophetic Ministry*, 2006. Used by permission.

[3] Todd Bentley, *Kingdom Rising: Making the Kingdom Real in Your Life*, (Shippensburg, PA: Destiny Image Publishers, 2008), p. 229.

## Chapter Two

[1] Biblesoft's *New Exhaustive Strong's Numbers and Concordance with Expanded Greek-Hebrew Dictionary*, Biblesoft, Inc. and International Bible Translators, 2006, NT: 4982.

[2] Dr. Bill Hamon, *Seventy Reasons for Speaking in Tongues*, (Shippensburg, PA: Destiny Image Publishers, 2012), p. 217.

[3] Biblesoft's *Strong's*, NT: 2842 Greek "koinwni/a (koy-nohn-ee'-ah); from NT:2844; partnership, i.e. (literally) participation, or (social) intercourse, or (pecuniary) benefaction.
KJV: (to) communicate (-ation), communion, (contri-) distribution, fellowship."

[4] Dick Purnell, *Knowing God by His Names: A Thirty-one Day Experiment*, (San Bernardino, CA: Here's Life Publishers, Inc., 1987), p. 11.

## Chapter Three

[1] Kay Arthur, *Lord I Want to Know You: A Devotional Study of the Names of God*, (Westwood, NJ: Fleming H. Revell Company, 1984).

## Chapter Five

[1] Biblesoft's *Strong's*, OT: 3073: "Hebrew...Yehovah Shalowm (yeh-ho-vaw' shaw lome); Jehovah (is) peace; *Jehovah-Shalom*, a symbolic name of an altar in Palestine: Jehovah-shalom."

## Chapter Six

[1] Jerome Groopman, M. D., *The Anatomy of Hope*, (New York, NY: Random House Trade Paperback, 2004), pp. 75-76.

[2] Beth Moore, *Believing God Workbook*, (Nashville, TN: LifeWay Press, 2002), p. 8.

## Chapter Seven

[1] There are two primary Greek words that are translated "word" in the New Testament: *logos* and *rhema*. Logos refers to "the total inspired Word of God and to Jesus, who is the living Logos." Rhema is "a verse or portion of Scripture that the Holy Spirit brings to our attention with application to a current situation or need for direction." From Advanced Training Institute International (https://atii.org>what is a rhema.)

[2] Charles Spurgeon, *Morning and Evening*, PC Study Bible, Version 5, formatted electronic database © 2006 by Biblesoft, Inc., Morning, April 28.

## Chapter Eight

[1] Biblesoft's *Strong's*, NT: 1411.
[2] Biblesoft's *Strong's*, NT: 450: "to stand up (literal of figurative, transitive or intransitive; KJV: arise, lift up, raise up (again), stand up (-right)."
[3] Biblesoft's *Strong's*, NT: 1849.

## Chapter Nine

[1] http://jonslack.blogspot.com/2010/01/amazing-report-from-nigeria.html
[2] Beth Moore, *Believing God*, (Nashville, TN: Broadman & Holman Publishers, 2004), p. 43.
[3] Perry Stone, *The Meal That Heals, Enjoying Intimate Daily Communion with God*, (Lake Mary, FL: Charisma House, 2008), p. 22.

## Chapter Ten

[1] https://www.facebook.com/nataliegrantmusic/posts/10156074770160421, January 10, 2018.
[2] http://smarturl.it/iTunesMoreThan

## Chapter Eleven and Chapter Twelve

[1] Phillip Keller, "A Gardener Looks at the Fruits of the Spirit," *Inspirational Writings*, (New York, NY: Inspirational Press, 1970), p. 474.
[2] Biblesoft's Spurgeon, *Morning*, June 21.

## Chapter Thirteen

[1] Henry Blackaby, *Experiencing God Workbook: Knowing and Doing the Will of God*, (Nashville, TN: LifeWay Press, 1990), p. 87.
[2] Biblesoft's Spurgeon, *Morning*, October 29.
[3] Blackaby, p. 42.
[4] Beth Moore, *Stepping Up, A Journey Through the Psalms of Ascent*, (Nashville, TN: LifeWay Press, 2008), p. 9.
[5] C. H. Spurgeon, *The Practice of Praise, How to Develop the Habit of Abundant, Continual Praise in Your Daily Life*, (Pittsburgh, PA: Whitaker House, 1995), p. 67.
[6] Stephen and Alex Kendrick, *The Battle Plan for Prayer*, (Nashville, TN: B&H Publishing Group, 2015).
[7] Biblesoft's Spurgeon, *Morning*, February 19.

## Chapter Fourteen

[1] Rick Warren, *The Purpose Driven Life*, (Grand Rapids, Michigan: Zondervan, 2002).
[2] Ibid., p. 282.
[3] Ibid., p. 282.
[4] Richard Nelson Bolles, *What Color is Your Parachute? 2020*, Appendix A: "Finding Your Mission in Life," (Berkeley, CA: Ten Speed Press, 2019).
[5] O. Carl Simonton, M. D. and Reid Henson, *The Healing Journey, The Simonton Center Program for Achieving Physical, Mental and Spiritual Health*, (New York, NY: Bantam Books, 1992), p. 53.
[6] http://www.stress.org.
[7] Norman Cousins, *The Healing Heart*, (New York, NY: W. W. Norton & Co., 1983), p. 33.
[8] Simonton, pp. 126, 54, 105-108.
[9] Bob Buford, *Half Time, Changing Your Game Plan from Success to Significance*, (Grand Rapids, Michigan: Zondervan Publishing House, 1994).
[10] http://nbcsports.com/video/steelers-james-conner-cancer-survivor-wouldnt-change-thing November 25, 2017
[11] Biblesoft's Spurgeon, *Morning*, February 19.
[12] Blackaby, p. 42.
[13] Kristina Brode of Germany as quoted in Simonton, *Healing Journey*, p. 11.

[14] Stone, p. 105.

[15] Michael Korda, *Man to Man, Surviving Prostate Cancer*, (New York, NY: Random House, 1996), p. 251.

[16] Biblesoft's *Strong's*: NT 1.

[17] Ibid., NT: 5598.

[18] Ibid., NT: 3144.

[19] Ibid., NT: 4393, 4253, 5342, and 4396.

[20] Bill Johnson, *YouTube*, "Power of the Testimony," September 30, 2009.

[21] Biblesoft's Spurgeon, *Morning*, April 16.

# BIBLIOGRAPHY

Bentley, Todd. *Christ's Healing Touch, Volume 1.* Canada: Sound of Fire Productions, 2004.

Blackaby, Henry T. & King, Claude V. *Experiencing God Workbook: Knowing and Doing the Will of God.* Nashville, TN: LifeWay Press, 1990.

Bodishbaugh, Signa. *The Journey to Wholeness in Christ.* Grand Rapids, MI: Chosen Books, 1997.

Bolles, Richard Nelson. Appendix A: "Finding Your Mission in Life" in *What Color is Your Parachute? 2020.* Berkley, CA: Ten Speed Press, 2019.

Breathnach, Sarah Ban. *The Simple Abundance Journal of Gratitude.* New York, NY: Warner Books, Inc., 1996.

Buford, Bob. *Halftime: Changing your Game Plan from Success to Significance.* Grand Rapids, MI: Zondervan, 1994.

Colbert, Don, M.D. *Let Food Be Your Medicine*, Dietary Changes Proven to Prevent or Reverse Disease. Brentwood, TN: Worthy Books, 2016

___*The New Bible Cure for Cancer: A Dietary Answer.* Lake Mary, FL: Siloam, 2010.

___ *Walking in Divine Health.* Lake Mary, FL: Creation House, 1999.

Copeland, Germaine. *Prayers That Avail Much, Volumes 1, 2 and 3.* Tulsa, OK: Harrison House, 1997.

Cousins, Norman. *The Healing Heart.* New York, NY: W.W. Norton & Co., 1983.

Groopman, Jerome, M.D. *The Anatomy of Hope.* New York, NY: Random House Trade Paperback, 2004.

Hamon, Dr. Bill. *Seventy Reasons for Speaking in Tongues.* Shippensburg, PA: Destiny Image, 2012.

Johnson, Bill. *YouTube*: "Power of the Testimony," September 30, 2009.

Kendrick, Stephen and Alex. *The Battle Plan for Prayer.* Nashville, TN: D & H Publishing Group, 2015.

Korda, Michael. *Man to Man: Surviving Prostate Cancer.* New York, NY: Random House, 1996.

Lawrence, Brother. *The Practice of The Presence of God.* Charlotte, NC: It's Supernatural and Messianic Vision, Inc., 2019.

Liardon, Roberts. *God's Generals.* New Kensington, PA: Whitaker House, 1996.

MacNutt, Francis, o. p. *Healing.* Notre Dame, Indiana: Ave Maria Press, 1974.

Manning, Brennan. *All Is Grace.* Colorado Springs, CO: David C. Cook, 2011.

Marshall, Catherine. *Adventures in Prayer.* Old Tappan, NJ: Chosen Books, 1975.

Moore, Beth. *Believing God.* Nashville, TN: Broadman and Holman Publishers, 2004.

___ *Believing God Workbook.* Nashville, TN: LifeWay Press, 2002.

___*Stepping Up: A Journey Through the Psalms of Ascent.* Nashville, TN: LifeWay Press, 2008.

Nee, Watchman. *A Living Sacrifice.* Hollis, NY: Christian Fellowship Publishers, 1972.

Ruth, Peggy Joyce and Schum, Angelia Ruth. *Psalm 91: God's Shield of Protection* (Military Edition). Not to be sold. Copies available from: info@1687foundation.com; 2005, 2007, 2009.

Omartian, Stormie. *Lord, I Want to Be Whole.* Nashville, TN: Thomas Nelson Publishers, 2000.

Prince, Derek. *Spiritual Warfare.* New Kensington, PA: Whitaker House, 1987.

Savard, Liberty. *Shattering Your Strongholds.* Gainesville, FL: Bridge-Logos, 1992.

Scanlan, Michael. *Inner Healing.* Paramus, NJ: Paulist Press, 1974.

Sherman, Dean. *Spiritual Warfare for Every Christian.* Seattle, WA: YWAM Publishing, 1990.

Sherrer, Quin and Garlock, Ruthanne. *A Woman's Guide to Spiritual Warfare*. Ventura, CA: Regal, 2010.

Simonton, O. Carl, M.D. and Henderson, Reid. *The Healing Journey: The Simonton Center Program for Achieving Physical, Mental, and Spiritual Health*. New York, NY: Bantam Books, 1992.

Smalley, Gary and Trent, John. *The Blessing*. New York, NY: Pocket Books, 1986.

Spurgeon, C. H. *The Practice of Praise: How to Develop the Habit of Abundant, Continual Praise in Your Daily Life*. Pittsburgh, PA: Whitaker House, 1995.

Stapleton, Ruth Carter. *The Experience of Inner Healing*. Waco, TX: Word Books, 1977.

___ *The Gift of Inner Healing*. Waco, TX: Word, Inc., 1976.

Stone, Perry. *Exposing Satan's Playbook*. Lake Mary, FL: Charisma House, 2012.

___ *The Meal That Heals: Enjoying Intimate Daily Communion with God*. Lake Mary, FL: Charisma House, 2008.

Wagner, C. Peter. *Warfare Prayer*. Ventura, CA: Regal Books, 1992.

Warren, Rick. *The Purpose Driven Life*. Grand Rapids, MI: Zondervan, 2002.

Wommack, Andrew, *The Believer's Authority: What You Didn't Learn in Church*. Tulsa, OK: Harrison House, 2009.

Wright, Henry. *A More Excellent Way: A Teaching on the Spiritual Roots of Disease*. Thomaston, GA, 2000.

Author Contact
trudybrinlinggoerk.com
for
*Patient's Guide to Cancer Overcomers,*
A *free* Booklet,
for the patient while going through active treatment:
*The Cancer Overcomers:*
*Your Healing Pathway*
*and*
*Your Testimony in the Making,*
*Book Two.*

CPSIA information can be obtained
at www.ICGtesting.com
Printed in the USA
JSHW031159220722
28402JS00007B/31